MW00328491

Arts & Sciences

also by ALBERT GOLDBARTH

Ontario Review Press Poetry Series

ARTS
&
SCIENCES

poems by
Albert Goldbarth

Ontario Review Press / Princeton

Library of Congress Cataloging in Publication Data

Goldbarth, Albert.
Arts & sciences.

(Ontario Review Press poetry series)
I. Title. II. Series.
PS3557.O354A89   1986   811'.54   86-12493
ISBN 0-86538-056-2
ISBN 0-86538-057-0 (pbk.)

Distributed by Persea Books, Inc.
225 Lafayette St.
New York, NY 10012

ACKNOWLEDGMENTS

Most of these poems were originally published in literary journals. To the editors of the following, my gratitude: *The American Poetry Review* ("Tarpan and Aurochs"), *The Beloit Poetry Journal* ("Hunt," "Knees/Dura-Europos"), *The Black Warrior Review* ("The Theory of Absolute Forms," "The Poem of the Praises"), *The Carolina Quarterly* ("The Ways and Means Committee," "Cathay"), *New England Review / Bread Loaf Quarterly* ("Khirbet Shemá," "The Elements," "'A Deep and Craving Hunger...for the Past'"), *The Ohio Review* ("Personal"), *The Ontario Review* ("U," "A Book About Rembrandt," "Second Level," "Matchbox"), *Parnassus* ("Paolo Uccello"), *Poetry* ("Vestigial," "'We're Just About to Observe the Edge of the Universe,'" "Problem Solving," "'The Numbering at Bethlehem,'" "Poem Whose Last Sentence Is 17 Syllables..."), *Shenandoah* ("A Window Seat," "Neologisms"), *Telescope* ("Wings"), *Tendril* ("Reading In"), *Three Rivers Poetry Journal* ("Dürer").

"Vestigial," "'The Numbering at Bethlehem,'" and "A Window Seat" were reprinted in *New American Poets of the 80's* (ed. Myers and Weingarten), Wampeter Press.

A fellowship from the John Simon Guggenheim Memorial Foundation enabled the writing and compiling of this manuscript.

with thanks to David Clewell and John Crisp,
fellow idlers

*How these curiosities would be quite forgott, did
not such idle fellowes as I am putt them downe.*
—John Aubrey

———————

*What the Boy chiefly dabbled in was natural history
and fairy tales, and he just took them as they came,
in a sandwichy sort of way, without making any
distinctions; and really his course of reading strikes
one as rather sensible.*
—Kenneth Grahame

CONTENTS

Some Science

Tarpan and Aurochs

In certain cases, it is possible to recreate extinct animals through careful breeding of present-day species. Two species that have been successfully recreated are a type of wild horse and a prototypical form of cattle.
—The World Almanac Book of the Strange #2

Eventually you'll be called. It will be
over water, or will appear to be
over a great expanse of water, no matter
where you are: the passage will be dark
with just a far, red rind of light that seems
to say an unseen shore. It may not be
a "shore," but water comes to mind, and
fish: some matrix-you, an early time of day
or life: a place that's amniotic. There's something calling
—your name, you think. And you hear it as if
over water. It will happen, and it will happen to you
in just this way. —Your real name, who you were
all along. Hoof-in-the-walking, Horn-from-the-skull,
Small-chain-of-original-protein.

*

In the subway car, peripheral vision flickers
unexpectedly with the B-train on the next track over
starting up, so giving you that second's (or less) illusion of
backwards travel. Travel backwards,
then: a blurred face in a length of A-train
rewound like a film. Who hasn't once
seen skydivers rise like that, the 'chutes above them
closing like flowers photography's run wrongway, then finally
folding like flowers, compactly back into the seed
—and not imagined himself in the car that tunnels
retrograde through time, to be the string
of metabolic process not yet even hard-wired
into the neural circuits, not yet even fetal REM, for which
midwifery hands are so macroscopic they don't exist.

*

There are paintings in which the souls of men are
breaking out of their bodies and rising like steam
from warm, torn bread, like steam with a very
calm face—and you see the painters really
believed in this, along with gold and rats
it's what the Middle Ages was all about.
The point of view is almost that of the souls'
—the flesh we take for granted, so everything paint
can mean to semblance is given to spirit's
verisimilitude. Finally, looking long enough,
the opposite occurs: it's the bodies of men we need
convincing of—did we really belong
to those things on the ground? (A waft, a spark,
is enough now.) Could such rough husks be ancestral?

*

I said *fetal REM*. The friend of a friend has found
the migratory stopping-place for North America's
monarchs: in the mountains north of Mexico City
37,000,000 drowse in conifers, one dun molecule or two of
thorax-susurration away from not being
anything at all. After sex, a lady asks
how many butterflies one of our heartbeats
could power. I turn to her not even knowing
the width of the border between a man and a woman
—slickness atoms-thick? or something so
large as prehistory and we'll never cross it
in this life? That the fetus's eyelids correspond
to one of those idling butterflies, I know, the way
we all know the travel of light though perhaps not its formula.

*

4

There's no measure for that distance. —But
you. Eventually you'll be called; you'll go, and be
a standard unit through incredible space. No
I don't want to turn from the pleasures of mattress,
glass, the well-bound book, the well-glazed duck
l'orange with almond slivers, electrical pylon
softened in morning snow, the nylon bunched about
her toes then straightened transparently over a thigh...
But we'll be called, so must prepare; must even
understand our hands on rocks, in sun, regress
to lizards; even learn to love the light the way the nuclei
of algae do, entire; even learn to love the dust and
even the subatomic bones of the dust; and make
the tarpan and aurochs, name them, know them eye to eye.

Vestigial

1. *Appendix, Coccyx, Pineal Eye*

Yes: that fingery fraction of a rabbit's commodious
sack, for the slow incorporating of cellulose: is
with us. The slinky bone-links of a tail have fused like flutes
into a panpipes: and are with us. And the lizard's
third, glazed eye is, like a whole yolk, folded
deep in the dough of our brains: and is awake there when
its outer brothers drowse. And there are some of us with
the tent-flap vestige of vaginal lips around the standard
penis; with three-teated breasts... Or the One and a
Halfs: with parasite baby-"brother" or -"sister" bodies
dangling partway out: Laloo the Hindu: arms,
waist, buttocks, legs "and perfect nails on the feet" extending forever
from his chest like a child burrowing in him, the head already
whispering to his lungs; it could pee and get hard. And
saying "freak" of them can't naysay what the gill and apehair
stages of the womb mean: everybody's wagged the tag-end of a fish
in the motherly waters. Do we know it, do we dream
the dreams of penguin, ostrich, rhea, kiwi, cassowary,
moa, rail, kakapo: all, birds for which flying's
a pair of muscley nubbins itching the living flesh.

2. *The Adventures of John Dee*

Not that an omelet of ostrich eggs intensifies
our own ties to the psyche of that African bird. Or
would he have thought exactly that?—John Dee,
astrologer and mage to the court of Elizabeth, himself
the wide-eyed vestige of an older world where poesie
and scientific method were a single creature romping
under planets, seraphs, meteor showers, ghosts. He
conjured ghosts. The Prince of Portugal ate ostrich eggs and
gave the shells to study: they were painted with the travel
of the heavenly spheres as agreeably authored by God and
telescope observation. Newton was around the corner.
Dee created a series of ten enormous "moonlight
towers," flashing war news for the Emperor Rudolph all
the way to Prague. And when the last faint light was

understood, and then slipped off its mirror, what did Dee think
in a darkened room of scrolls and crystals? Aubrey was around
the corner, scrutinizing megaliths. This final moment
Stonehenge still might be the footstools giants left. Dee
lifted a dinosaur bone. It might be Noah's, he thought, this
trace of a time when stature matched faith and accomplishment.

3. *Big Bang*

Ooohing over Stonehenge—over skew-silhouetted
Egyptian gods, or Hopi sand mandalas—finally
recognizes not what's different but what's essentially
us in them. And so we flock to Laloo and his atavistic cohorts,
Alligator Lady, Monkey Boy, to see their fairground skins containing
ordinary life. They wink and sip their scotch. They marry. When
The Human Frog and Mule Woman wed, Sabine the Serpent Girl was
maid of honor—then godmother seven times. They only made the same
attempt as anyone you know, to be the wheel Plato says
we all were in the days when man and woman formed a single-bodied
being rolling breezily over the world. I think that's why
at night, some nights, we see the stars in their terrible solitude
and systems of attachment: as a sign for what our lives are:
smithereens on fire, having been exploded from our wholeness
and our source. That may be accurate cosmology or not. I
only know I've walked the darkness wanting more than any
Stonehenge to align with something bright. And then the lunar
dole of remnant sunlight touched me—here: an x between
the shoulderblades, those made-for-raising things. They stirred. Not
wings, no. More like the fossils of wings.

"We're Just About to Observe the Edge
of the Universe"

he says in the kitchen. Everywhere else
the party is tightening, couples in the livingroom
dancing progressively closer and even former strangers
at the coldcuts table exhibit the minimal group cinch
of a conversation working like a drawstring. Here,
we're with the galaxies. Flying apart,
continuously, at speed that smears the light
the speed is seen by. "And when they reach what we call
'the event horizon' they disappear. They go over
the bounds of our visual capability. For us that's the edge
of anything knowable." G. with her drink
held hard in her hands, like a votive candle.
Dick backed to a row of silver ladles. "We think
the new 300-incher is going to focus that in."
At dark, in West Texas' Davis Mountains,
the deer and the brush and the hunter-tongued lizards
all the color *night*, they're going to funnel the finalmost photons in
from the definite end of everything, so no wonder
the copper napkin rings, the cups, the tureen of pinto beans
simmering: sweet heaped details, holding us firm.

*

The ceiling is the sky, and in some of the more elaborate
pyramid chambers, intricate astral maps are in relief
above the dead. The wall is the world, this world, for taking
with completely. The tomb of Djehuty-nekht is painted
with a lion-headed bed, its linen cover folded
neatly on top. There are headrests of cedar and alabaster,
a copper dagger, a white papyrus fan (sketched in with
gray detail as fine as for the individual overlaying
tufts of a wing), four ceremonial vases of faience and gold,
an offering table with oval honey-cakes and animal heads,
a cowhide-covered spear-case tilted casually
against its wooden stand as if set down just now
with the damp of the river still on it, pouches of eye-paint
(olive and jet), a mirror, an apron, this is a house, the house
of eternity they called it. And when a life approached

8

the edge of life, and drew a final breath and went
out of our range, beyond the most advanced reception, it
continued in another universe held by the solids
of this one. There are extra sickles and writing-palettes in case
the originals wear smooth being used in eternity.

*

We've talked cosmology, cocaine, the skiing season,
Elizabeth Bishop's poems, the flat stacking-up
of Egyptian frieze... Now G. just wants the sideboard.
"That's all. The rest he can have. The dachshunds even."
She went to the Judy Collins concert, alone, and wept
at their favorite songs. She's thinking of calling the lawyer.
In the livingroom now it's 20's music; the final, fine-tuned
calibrations of intimacy are slow-danced cheek
to cheek, each couple's various sweats from the cajun records
drying into a single salt-based glaze. We step
outside. The stars have also aligned into shapes for spending
the night together. Dipper, Scales, Net and Cup play house
in the middle of nothing, and it works for the little
while it's needed. Now Morgan joins us. The three of us breathing
outside in, its rough cool touch and the lungs' accommodation.
"The sideboard's beautiful really." Really we can imagine
the life on another planet so far, so long
divorced from our system, it doesn't even recognize the objects
we hang on those scintillant pegs,
the saving array of a household.

The Theory of Absolute Forms

It isn't easy to picture an infinite universe,
a star that's travelling through an infinite universe,
but think of how far pain can go in your bone,
in its marrow. —Forever, I think. When Plato
clutched his side and moaned, he knew how this world's
hurt is only the light from its star Generic Hurt.

*

Say I have a wound like a flamenco beauty's horrible
red camelia set in my flesh. I think the doctor's
whole career has been for this moment. The wound,
my wound, it's only been with me an hour.
His hands are exact. They lift it and dance.
He's been intimate with this wound for years.

Personal

A rorschach "has" meaning. It's something like a rorschach,
this symmetrical abstraction on a tortoise belly, blackish
jade on buff. And Darwin hunkers alongside it, moved and
unmoving all afternoon. Whatever it means, by evening
when he walks back through the islands' arduous air, it's
some jade puzzle-part of evolution. We learned that

in Science. In those days, 8th grade, everything that happened
had a message. It wasn't only that every flowerhead said
a seraglio to Linnaeus, or every star was a passionate courier
from the universe to Galileo. It wasn't just school. By
day, each weed, each birdshit-chalky fireplug, each impossibly
poignant salute of a skirt in the breeze, was untranslatable

profundities about who I was. And at dusk,
my future took place in the dark between the tv flicking
to life like the bulb in the rabbi's lectern, and all of the far
congregational stars arriving to sing amen at the speed of light.
When there isn't difference between the world and
autobiography, each stone "means." What's strange is,

there was a woman I mistreated—really a girl, or whatever
one is in 8th grade History. She wept. And *that* meant
nothing to me; I was still between a boy
and a man. The class was between the first and second
Wars; we researched a paper on "Germany's Reparations" together,
necking, obdurate, cruel. I may have wept as well. It's

late by 20 years but I want to make reparation too,
to Leah... her surname I forget, it spoke of passage
in steerage, candle rituals, *kosherkeit*, -baum or -berg.
I want to make reparation to, and through, this girl to dozens
I've wronged—and you do too. Religion, psychiatry,
know, and fatten off, that. Look, we'll make a deal:

11

when I say "now" we'll merely turn from this story and be
good to some other person. It's really that simple. My writing
this sentence and your reading it is our contract, ok? Ok, so
you've agreed. Because the filament of a single 3-inch silkworm
runs a mile, because the edge of an usher-torn concert ticket is
worthy of Rand-McNally annotation, it was easier to hurt people

in 8th grade: everywhere we stared we found a bounty we
thought made for us alone, so pain in everybody else was peripheral
and, in any case, healable by their own rich monogrammed cosmos. I
believed our griefs were effortlessly given consolation by
the text in any brick or cloud or bough. But then History
showed us some photos—mass bulldozered graves—and

I'm not sure I believe that now.

Khirbet Shemá

Because I lost the captions, this aerial view
of an ancient synagogue's toppled columns
and this close-in shot of unearthed pottery beads

are indistinguishable—the tubular beads
in magnification as gray as the gray stone tons,
and casting equally credible shadow: relativity

not wholly unlike something taking shape
as Einstein sits in a fanning of secular light
through the doorpane on Yom Kippur. I

don't want to cheapen his thought or turn it
whimsical. But the light takes the form
of a woman, collects into jawline and breasts,

a loveliness from another time, the way
light's saved in a camera. I have a photograph
of someone who made a poignant faith

in dailiness, its labors and its unaccountable
happiness, take place in me—but she's
almost indistinguishable,

now, in the gray, from the tumbled architecture
of Khirbet Shemá. I think about
its crumbled rock faces increasingly; with every day

away from the year 400, its ritual bath,
bone piles and Torah shrine are clearer
in my mind—exactly the opposite

from a Renaissance master's lessons
in perspective. The farther away,
the larger. That's a definition

of God, of course. Why not? I'll never know
the convolutedness of Einstein's mind but
I can tell you this: he sees her

13

clasp the beads—some have an acronymic scripture
going round—and they ride like gray buoys
on the pulses of her throat. But when he tries

to test the substance of her cheek—or maybe
he only wants a tenderness—she's gone.
It's the holiest day of the year. She

stops outside the synagogue and a cry
of penitential request escapes her, that
or a song of great joy. It's relative, and

it's the same light, either way, she feels lift her.

Problem Solving

*. . . [Leonardo] persuaded the Florentine Government—probably
the most hard-headed body in Europe—to accept his design for
diverting the Arno so that it should no longer enter the sea by
Pisa, but in Florentine territory.*
                              —Kenneth Clark

From a knoll above the Arno he watches its muscular washes work
a crook of bank glass-smooth. The light he's made display
the pages' peach-cheeked cherubs, complicated lanyarding
of tendons up the haunch of a lynx, convenings of saints, latches
of crab and beetle, drills the size of market bulls for breaching
bolted castle gates, and the exact if casual fall of folds
in linen (or beldam neck-wattles): shadows
and clarifies his own face now, makes of him a focusing
of planes above the clean thrust of the river. And how
to channel it? and measure its drive? and capture every
evanescent tiara of froth, in charcoal? You see, there
exist many problems. It's 1503. An easy ride away,

inside a shadowy room in a ramshackle twist of the city,
another man, who faces what looks like crisis, maybe *because*
he faces what looks like crisis, flashes for seconds back
to the one-man-band he made of himself in his 10th year,
with a row of Mama's good Venetian flasks, and each its
own tone in a tavern song, from its own noted level of water.
Because of him—you'll see why—I think of my sister.
It's 1983. She calls to say they're back from the last
swell-bellied Lamaze class (Bobby coaching at her
hillocky side as she practices the rapid, pursed,
prescriptual breathing of what the nomenclature labels
"Easing"). Their dry run's flawless. This is birthing's better

15

mousetrap. Plastic food wrap, multinational embargo,
the periodic table of elements, divorce court, and those
bath mats with the rows of rubber suction cups are
answers, and the simple truth is every question's simple
when it's solved. And so a sculptor ransacks attic clutter
again for the tin with her daughter's confirmation tresses
saved inside, and these become the model used for 18 feet
of marble water slipping over a falls-lip, straight
through marble air, and hitting in a beautiful welter of marble
curl on curl. We're each of us 90% composed of that
element Leonardo's studying so avidly as it ravels its lavish way
to the sea—and some nights, late, out walking trouble off, I

know I could picture the blue-gray bends of vein in the wrists
or necks of friends, with all of the finicky passion he fit
to the level of hydrodynamics: floodgate, basin, sluice.
Now down the full canals of my sister's body I'm wishing an easy
delivery. Tubeways, ducts, the dark infolding bays: his
sketches of the fetus make a lucid vision, yet re-redraft
his map of the Arno's flow till the sun's so low it's red and
Leonardo's still not wholly satisfied but dawdles home with the itch of it
bearing down. Across town, another man sees shadows say
it's late, and still the midwife isn't come. It's 4 long
centuries before Lamaze, but *here, blow into the bottle* he says. She
does. Like he did as a kid. The bag of waters

bursts. Breath. Bottle. *Easy...* A great note of music is born.

Lindsay Nichol Baran,
May 27, 1983

*Leonardo's map of the river
networks of Tuscany would become
"the first modern map in Western
history"* (H.F. Judson)

The Ways and Means Committee

Ways

August night. The hot kind where the air's like soup, the air at your mouth's like fat around the soupbone.

So I'm out of bed, I'm sitting in a dark house under half-a-gram of undiluted starlight. From a dark block over, the phlegmy low of 16-wheelers, then that sound's drowned by a jet's. I always think their kind of noise should leave a mark across the sky, like a sharpedged pebble over glass. Another one follows in less than ten minutes. This house must be along any number of transport lanes. Some late-nighter tootles his lowslung horn and a semi answers. A flying thing, blackish and fat, about the size of a small plum, buzzes the screen, then it's gone. I suddenly see all the routes—the world I live in is crosshatched, like an 18th-century etching, line of traffic and line of traffic and line, as fine as a screen—I might be a small life buzzing, myself.

"I was just a leaf, a little man-leaf, in comparison"—John writes from Hawaii. It's spring; the whale-ways are filling. Every year they stop to mate and give birth and sing in their soulful basso that the waters carry as air, the lighter medium, carries our lighter song. The largest blue can weigh as much as 25 bull elephants—four times more than the largest dinosaur known. The tongue is a mansion of fat. The skull is a mansion ballroom, with a small steady thought for a chandelier. And yet you should see their mating grace—two of them bobbing like hens' eggs in the water. A newborn clips to a honey-brown nipple, and its throat forms to its first two-gallon suck... The recitals of whales will vibrate the hull of your boat, then into your palm or your feet, and if you've dived into the water the air in your sinuses vibrates in sympathy; you float in that sapphire-blue—as sky or heaven, the lighter medium, is blue—and the naves and the chancels of your body come alive, and thrum the musics of that service, thrum and thrum. —"And I fluttered like a leaf."

This house, in fact, is stationed along the migration-ways of leaves as much as it is for any V of geese or any fleet of route-vans bringing Choco-bars and Ripple-chips to the emptying tracks of vending machines in the nooks of Interstate 80. Already, the leaves are hardening, yellowing toward brown. September will see the first great glide. And a few weeks after leaving Hawaii, the humpbacks are seen off the coast of Alaska, learning variations on their beautiful blubbery themes.

The only difference is, the migration of geese is chiefly in distance; of trees, chiefly in ways of being. I don't know how long, exactly, it takes those determined Canadian flyers to make it back north every spring. I do know it took three unaccountable months for John's Hawaii letter to reach this everyday Midwest address. There must be any number of vast invisible grids of disappearance, hiatus potholes, lacuna hotels, in any viable, long-used travel lane—though the Post Office probably demonstrates this best. But where does the God of Spring go, seeing his whole green purview brittle and chill? Does He lay Him down in a bed constructed of whales' giant leg bones—where they went to when they disappeared, leaving only some knuckle-sized nubbins buried deep in the hips. Where does consciousness go? The geese settle down. Each folds its sleek head under a wing. I'm sleepy, myself. The stubby wing I have is a plastic toggle, set in a plastic plaque—I've turned it on, it's straight out for this stubby illumination, and soon I'll flick it down and off and lay my head on feathers, in dark. Hello, God. Hello, many Gods.

John now in Canada fishing for muskie... Morgan here in the other room with her pillow under her arm like an attaché case carrying dream ... Alane... Tony... A truck moans. Then my body in bed. Another access ramp, in this city of access ramps, to the main ways.

Means

In those laborious 19th-century novels, a chapter is given over to the letter's composition, by guttering taper-light, and with many a detailed paragraph-long sigh. A while farther, a chapter is wholly dedicated to the letter's being read, a week later, with similar sighs in response—perhaps the same sighs?—maybe a letter then was a clever contrivance thought up for absorbing, condensing, transporting and then releasing a sigh from an orifice for sighs that someone else, at this climactic moment, might call rosebud lips...

But there is no chapter devoted to such surmise. Nor is there a chapter on the mail coach, the means, although its fraying leather reins and crusted wheels and stops at the trashdump doors of inns, its horses breathing through the humid night like kettles and with a kettle's insistent whistle, its fleas and its grease... are the ecology, machinery and intermediate language of the letter's being conveyed, are what makes anything of narrative consequence possible.

Nor is there the novel on the taper's transition. We wake up one day in the 20th century, people in books are phoning each other, sighing then rapidly phoning each other, though first they turn on the light.

*

When I was very young—and I'd always be hopeless with engineering matters like getting an oven lit or a car hood open—I fantasized two molecule-sized people lived in a light bulb, and rubbed each other, and by some magical Boy and Girl Scout friction, threw off watts.

I still tend to believe in that theory. I can understand my finger lazily flicking the lamp switch, I can understand its result: the bed I'm sitting up writing in fills with light. But I can never fully comprehend the river between those two, the hundreds of miles of flowing under stars to turn the hydropower stations. I've seen, but can't quite place in my world, the generating tunnels large enough to hold a man, the maze of generating tunnels connecting in cities that spark while the rest of us sleep, transformers, and three-phase tension circuits, and solenoid oil circuit breakers, the massive towers and underground banks, the roomsfull of convolute feed lines...

With all that apparatus ready, we still haven't fixed up the attic with outlets. Sometimes we bring flashlights there; more often than not, just candles. And the photos, too, say an earlier time. My parents are stiff signs in sepia meaning *love* or *fun* or *showiness*, though some don't read too clearly over the years. And here's their wedding. They're not even two inches high—from picture to picture, posing with this guest, posing with that—small, interchangeable parent-parts. The molecule people, the source of it all, the ones inside who made the light.

Not that I'd want to push such slight analogy with too much force— my life as the product of hydroelectric transmission. Though *Albert* does mean *bright*, or *shining*. And I've seen my friend Mimi Bardagjy give birth. She was awake and pushing knowledgeably, and Michael was with her, breathing along in great guiding sounds—much different I'm sure than it was for my mother Fannie Seligman Goldbarth in Mt. Sinai Hospital, January 1948 with the blizzard outside and her brain knocked cold by an injection. Then the blood, and the bursting of waters, and the opening up of the under-room, the place of generation—large, enough to hold a man—and the slippery paying out of the feed lines...

*

Did I write in a letter that "Mimi gave the baby his initiating suck this morning, her face all glowing?" And did I mean it? *Glowing?*

Did the breasts of Anna Monaro glow blue as she slept? They did, Italian medical journals say they did in May of 1934, and "Dr. Protti made a long statement on his observations." Gould and Pyle tell of a woman whose breast emitted light enough by which to read the hands of a watch "several feet away." And did Caroline Clare of London, Ontario discharge electrical power? In the summer of 1879 the Ontario Medical Association reported fully credulously that "cutlery would stick to her skin and her corset stays became magnetized." And the baby born in Saint-Urbain, France in 1869 whose fingers shot luminous rays and who "shocked all who touched him"? The baby whose touch was able to charge up a Leyden jar? How much do we know, do we really know, of the tubes in the tubes of the body? High-voltage photography produces an image of objects—including animate objects—surrounded by a luminescent aura. Plants and human fingerprints give off wavery ribbons of reds and icy whites like the Northern Lights in small-town Minnesota that first time, running naked out of the tent and falling wild-eyed into a sexual hug

20

with the whole night sky shooting glory. And then did you tell each other your faces glowed? And then was the Buddha like unto a candle? And then did the high-voltage photographs of leaves both living and fallen become a definitive study and then did Moses come down from the mount, from Sinai, but he wist not that the skin of his face did shine, and all beheld it, so that in speaking to the Children he need put on a veil, but when he went before the Lord to speak, he took him the veil off.

*

Under my father's boyhood Bible, then under the Boy Scout badges, then under that brittling miscellany of documentation from almost any family's storage, is a string-tied bundle of love letters to the woman who'd be my mother. They're embarrassing, and lovely. *Thought of you and blushed at Miltie's... No night in the bomber raids could make my heart thump so...* They speak of things so lost they could be archeologist's prizes. They're transmitters of sighs, as baked clay pots were transmitters of water. *Say yes. I want to put your name on the marquee of The Rialto and let it burn through the night.* The lights of another time. The things they shone for.

How much do we know of the tubes in the tubes? Of the Turin shroud? Of a single quill pen in a cedar chest from the early 1700's? Of how we arrive *here, now?* In 1936 William Koenig, a German archeologist in Iran, was shown an object supposedly dug from the earth at Khujut Rabu'a, an ancient village near Baghdad. It was an earthenware vase with a copper cylinder, looking like a battery cell. It could have worked as a battery cell. Evidence exists of what might be electroplating on copper vases from 2500 B.C. There are drawings on walls from then we still can't read, long letters to God or amatory verses to somebody's rosebud lips. And this could be a battery cell from the year of Christ's birth. Miltie's. The Rialto. Nobody knows what it means.

It's difficult, *not* to see birds as those lyrically-scripted w's and m's across the skies of our childhood drawings. The clouds were clumps of mashed potatoes, the sun was a perfect gold yolk, and birds in the distance were always writing, www and mmm, in black lines on sky-blue. I lived in Chicago. They were crows, I'm sure, though none of us had ever seen a crow, just pigeons and sparrows. They were crows, and they were approaching with their raucous partying caws. I can't prove this. Objectively you look at those tiny black moustaches and epaulettes in flight above the crayon hills, and there's no way to prove they aren't leaving, tinier each moment. *Flight* even tells us this—a fugitive's in flight, away from. But I'm convinced that when I drew them year after year, when all of my hundreds of classmates over the years would draw them, page on page, those birds were meant to be approaching, those birds were the right to assemble, these were loud American birds, this was a convention and constituent birds of the One True Bird were flocking to town left and right. That alphabetical image seems accurate today; I look out this meetingroom window at passing birds and think if I could freeze-frame what I see I'd have a square with wedgy chevron-shapes across it, like nothing so much as a clay accounting-tablet, from Uruk, 8000 years ago. It's one of the things we have that says behind it there was settlement, ownership, codes and specialization—what a city finally means instead of wandering, what congregation does. It tells us mud-brick walls and fenced grain, says community. Not all of these earliest records are readable now. Because of those that are—because of what we know ourselves to be, with papers in front of us, an agenda to follow, a window to our left that snags attention—we intuit the content of many of these documents: the usual muddle of getting-things-done: that a punishment be meted out, that a price be set, that a sticky decision be tabled. So familiar, I can see a scribe, in the terrible Middle East sun, just done with freshening his clay from a shallow water pan, and looking up amazed from his birdtrack writing, to that huge, exact, original V as it gathers itself overhead. When the leader veers the V veers, as if solid. It dips like a single light wing. No wonder he messes the meeting's meticulous minutes, tosses the slab to a side and starts over. Watching Greater Birds-of-Paradise display is like seeing a slower, clumsier version of in-flight groupwork. At dawn they rally in the undergrowth. They have dragonfly-green necks, canary-yellow heads, brown backs and long gold and tangerine plumes. The first one flies up to the dance branch. He shrieks, bows, claps his wings overhead and fans his fiery plumage. The passion

22

catches—one by one they take turns on the dance branch, in exalting series. What if this took place in the air? What if this took place in the neurons? What if these birds were one lovely beast, made up of many decisions? That a boundary be extended, that a gap be tightened up, that a consensus shape from chaos. Birds sing in groups—three boubou shrikes in Uganda will keep their territories inviolate, but join in the same shrill song, each doing his part. It's been measured: in mating season, a catchy tune will travel at a fairly constant mile-and-a-half per day. Prairie dog towns are a thousand large; their sentries pop and duck in Busby Berkley coordination. Hyena packs team at their regular spot (an area marked by urine), lick each other's genitalia, let their blood tune to the same high crazy whine, then go for zebra in a single supple run of numerous units, at one command and with one hunger. Chimps will groom each other in chains six long, beyond the need for cleanliness, in friendship. That a limit be set, that a ruling be reached, that everything be ordered. Termites click together like tympani sections. Hierarchy of social rank exists in barnyard chicken coops. Three hundred thousand bats can circle blind in a room-sized cave and not once bump. We don't know how. But we'll discuss it, if there's a quorum here we'll discuss it. Human twins a thousand U.S. miles apart have waked at 9:07 (Rome time) when their mother's heart stopped beating. We don't know how, they don't know how, but it's being filibustered, it's a motion on the floor. The so-called "small world problem" states "a chain of only five friends will ulti-mately link up any two average individuals in the United States; and probably ten friends, any two on Earth." This was discovered in 1967, at Harvard. Fish are also a school. Hundreds glide then sweep sharp at an angle, like the thinking of one gray brain in the water; debate lasts the length of an atom. A school... I look out the window. A bird yoo-hoos. The leaves of a tree are adjourning... That a vote has been called, that a yes has been said, that we've met here again, in committee.

Hunt

A sheaf of some. Some (like Mrs. Browning's)
in the lavish concentrics of Moorish design.
George Washington's is a single fraying bangle.
Some are fish lures, in their thickness and gaudy loll.
Others, a minimal sprig of baby's-breath.
There are broomheads, and eddies, and elegant,
skaterly, bubble-chamber spirals

of hair. And Milton's occasions a sonnet
(There seems a love in hair, though it be dead.
It is the gentlest, yet the strongest, thread
Of our frail plant...). And sour Dean Swift is given
double entry *(His hair when old, and his hair*
when young). Also two locks from Keats. And each
appears with an engraving of the head where it first took
luxuriant root; and each is lovingly labeled
and dated in hand-done print as regimental as type;
and each, its history: Napoleon's, *Obtained*
from his hairdresser by Mrs. Leigh, who gave it to
her brother, Lord Byron, who gave it to

Leigh Hunt. Whose collection it is. Bound richly
in burgundy leather, with his likeness on the cover,
and sturdy, floral decoration intertwining
with the letters COLLECTION OF HAIR.
As we see him, he's going over his Milton sonnet, again,
again—almost, we want to say, "combing." *It*

lies before me there, and my own breath
Stirs its thin outer threads, as though beside
The living head I stood... The candle
glimmers off the pearl of his undone collar,
off his untouched wine. He's been in there hours.
He wants it ringing true.
He runs his hands through his hair.

––––––

24

These were the days of collecting.
Beetles. Fossils. Bottles. Oriental
sex prosthetics (ivory, lovely
eel-bodied and bullheaded things).
The yellowed slivers of saints. Hair. There,

they all arrived—the would-be great, and great—
in Leigh Hunt's study, and stayed
to talk of immortality, in one way or another.
Lamb was there, and Hazlitt. Jeremy Bentham
praised "the elephant's trunk, which lifts
alike a pin or twelve hundredweight." Byron

unwrapping the packet with Napoleon's few sad strands.
Coleridge. Wordsworth. Keats. The Shelleys
donated a lock apiece on 3 December 1820,
hers a particular beauty in its bountiful roundness.
These were the cast, or some of the cast, and as he collected
their minds in his editorial endeavors, he collected

odd personal bits: lace tatters, a vase, this straggle
snipped from Johnson's scalp *two days after death.*
Although at Shelley's cremation, Hunt
remained in the carriage. Byron asks for the skull—"but,"
Trelawny says of it, "remembering that he had formerly
used one as a drinking-cup," the poet is refused.
"The brains literally seethed, bubbled, and boiled
as if in a cauldron." Trelawny snatches the whole fat

heart from the ashes, and later presents it to Mary.
These are the pins. As for the hundredweight, Jeremy Bentham

"is preserved entire" at University College. To touch him.
Like stroking the fitted, mineral-black back
of a beetle, a something

out of its time, in our time. To touch him,
or any of them. Pinned in their cases,
bound in their books.
In the days of collecting, death
is only the last of the many anthologies.

———

To get it; to touch it; to bring forth from it
breath, or spark, or marrow,
in communion and possessorship.

And Milton they disinterred, some
necrokleptoretentive antiquarian ratsasses,
knocked the teeth out with a stone, then twisted
off a leg as if tearing small wood for the fire, and took
"a large quantity of the hair, which lay
straight and even, just as it had been combed and tied
together before interment."

To get it; to risk to get it; to get in the pit of it,
the yolk, the neural sanctorum, the pulse-dot, the sexual x;
to revere it; to brand your initials.

And Pope is composing a note in request of another
"hogshead of scallop shells." By night,
in the earliest days of its construction, he enters
his Grotto and dances, hunched back
in a stuttering candle, dances like a wild thing
through his wild collection: petrified moss,
marble from Rome, doves' eggs, gold and silver
in egg-sized workings of ore from Peru, "the usual
fossils and gems," "small stones, incrusted over,
out of the river Thames," flints, winter-hardened
animal tracks, bloodstones, snakestones, "two stones
from the Giant's Causeway," busts and urns
around the wall, "large clumps of Cornish diamonds,"
"Plates of Looking glass,"
heaped crystal, corals, pelts and claws, a hummingbird's nest.
"I must add, to my shame, I am one of that sort
who at his heart loves bawbles better [than riches]..."

To get it; to know it; to lay yourself along it
face to face; to name it; to place it; to be with it
atom attuned to atom, drug to bloodstream, stone to flesh.

And Shelley is worrying over where he's collected
the best of himself on paper. We'll know it as "Ode
to the West Wind." Here, today, the manuscript page
is titled "Octr 25." He scratches out *loose locks*
and now it's *bright hair*—this, so *The hair*
of the approaching storm can be *The locks*. He says it
aloud. He sings it. He taps it, to see if it finds a
concomitant tap of approval
from deep in the meat of his brain.

To get it;
but then to get it right.

———

In the days of collecting I searched
for the proper material, something,
anything: the albums of love,
the bright figurettes of the holy.

And in upstate New York, Mel Birnkrant returns
from whatever muddying up of a person the world can do
in a day, and opens the door on that recleansing he calls
home: it's Eunice Birnkrant and "more
than two thousand separate pieces of Mickey Mouse
memorabilia." What does he see, and become, staring out
of the windows of that world? Some nights the moon
must touch the fringe it makes of itself
in the delicate verticals of the Fingerlakes falls,
must touch the sharp white breakage it places
in tamarack tops, must jewel the lawns, with perfect
satiation. And he looks up, and the face he sees in that
fullness is his secret.

And Emanuele Litto Damonte,
the Pope Valley Hubcap King, holds court
in a "hubcap ranch" of over 3,000. He's 91.
"I just did it. People bring 'dem, and I
hang 'dem up. I'm Litto. I'm here.
'Dis is my place." And

Grandma Tressa Prisbey, 87, lives in Bottle Village:
22 buildings done, in their entirety, of bottles set in cement.
She walks with a cane now, and she can't much keep
the shining up. One building is called the Little Chapel,
one has goat skulls over the door. And why did she pour
her life in these bottles, these landfill castoffs
saved by her for infrastructure? "I did it to house
my pencil collection. I have more
than 10,000 pencils, you know."

I know. By such vicarious accumulation, mice
in felt and iron, everyone knows, and in the days
of collecting we walk with the burn of wanting our own
unbearable heaviness lightened
by itemization. The hill was a good place to stop,
so I stopped. The moon was a good thing to want,
so I howled. Or not the moon exactly,
no, but some idea of how a calendar could be made
from brightness's phases. And I didn't exactly
howl. I made the small, high sounds of wanting
to be touched by wanting—something,
anything. Hubcaps. Hair.

"I can remember that I was afraid of being left alone,
and that I was comforted by sitting in a Mickey Mouse chair
that was there... I love the innocence of that figure, I want

to see it restored to an active place in our lives."

———

By now the sky was green, a deepening
emerald-green, and he knew the storm was nearing.
He knew, as well, a half-smashed squatters' shack
lay an hour ahead, where they'd welcome him with their
empty-handed open-armed generous ways (as he
was welcome, in fact, at some of the best of the tended
estates in the colonies—even Mr. Custis once,
whose widowed daughter-in-law would marry
George Washington, hosted this "downright plain
country man" and they stayed up talking the cultivation
of mountain cowslip all night). But the shack

would be undulant in vermin; his horse
would mind the downpour less than an hour-more run;
and so he leisurely finished the last of the wood rat
(in honey and sour orange pulp: "a relishing morsel")
and rode out slow, to meet the rain with whatever
acceptance he'd learned from the wild greengrowing things,
seed and shoot and blossom, of his collecting

—John Bartram, that farmer from the banks
of the Kingsessing, who traveled two weeks for a few new
willow-leafed acorns. Who traveled the Dismal Vale,
the Endless Mountains, the Impenetrable Mountains,
the Rattlesnake Mountains, Flying Hill, Licking Place.
Up to Canada. Down to Florida. (And once, "as I was
walking in a path an Indian man met me and
pulled off my hat in a very great passion and
chewed it all round—I suppose to show me that they
would eat me if I came in that country again.") Who
came in that country again, who smudged himself his life long
in the natural mulch of that—his, ours,
this—country. John Bartram, collector

for Peter Collinson, London merchant and amateur
botanist. England crazy for New World flora. Bartram
by inches through its hills. "Pray send a root or two
of the glassy leaves that bear little blue flowers, that's
good against the obstruction of the bowels; and a good root
of Swallow-wort, and hop tree, allspice,
wild roses, and if thee observes any freshwater shell fish
or land snails..." He observed. He sent.
In glass jars filled with camphor. Or wrapped in damp moss.
The beetles and smaller animals crammed into jars
filled with rum (though sailors sometimes drank these).
Nuts were waxed. Tortoise-shell snuffboxes varnished
air-tight. In 40 years he introduced a full
one-fourth of the 600 native American plants
known in Europe. John Bartram. Collected

shooting star, white osier, bittersweet, steeplebush,
arrowroot, river birch, witch hazel, sassafras,
dogwood, sweet gum, hickory, hemlock, buttonbush,
sand myrtle, mayflower, cucumber, butterflies

arriving "a little torn," a box of turtle eggs
that hatched upon arrival "and then with their forefeet
scratched their eyes open," redwood, canewood,
life everlasting, "a monkfish having
a hood like a friar's cowl," wasp nests, and a tipitiwichet that "does
trap flies for devouring." Knew them. Loved them. Collection
shipment to shipment. And Collinson gave
some American seeds to "a universal lover of plants" and
eventual patron, Lord Petre,
                                          whose father
had clipped a snippet of hair off the head of his kinswoman
Arabella Fermor, thus inspiring
Pope to write *The Rape of the Lock.*

Something, anything. Rosebay. Laurel. Maple.
The mosses we now call *Bartramia.*
Hubcaps. Hair.

———————

To have it. To touch it. Jeremy
Bentham, say. The long-dead pemmican meat
and slowly browning bones of Jeremy Bentham on display.
To touch it, to love it, Aladdin
to lamp. How long did it take
for a genie? To touch it, to buff it, to bring it
to life, or a semblance of life, through attention.
I walked and I wanted it,
something... I often thought of a woman
asleep beside me. How I'd simply stroke her
hair, her hair like oceanwaves off the glaze
of a Japanese plate, such stylized ringleting, yes just
stroking it in the darkness, stroking a spark
alive in the oils of the interior, stroking a cobalt
crackle of lightning down the dark, to have it,
to touch it, to love it, to bring it to wholeness,
to stroke her awake.

On the 5th floor of the U of Texas Special Collections Library
is the "vertical file"—miscellaneous
junk-*cum*-exotica storage. What is it,
that asking for Leigh Hunt's catalogued compendium

should encourage an offer of being toured through this
mess of lesser literary curio-detritus:

John Masefield's teddybear "Bruno." Two
cigarette butts of John Cowper Powys's (June 7, 1939)
and a swatch of his hair. "Cuttings from Shaw's beard."
Whitman's hair (1890–92) and a gold pin
with a lock of hair at its heart. Stein's
waistcoat. Carson McCullers's nightgown. *All,*
both pellings at once: re-, com-. Poe's glasses.
The Coleridge family hair. And Arthur Conan Doyle's
cuesticks and golf clubs and hairbrush and
socks with a note: "The socks which were on
my Belovéd's feet—put on by the nurse after
he had passed on—Which I took off and replaced
others with my own hands." *I don't want to know.*

I want to know. Robinson Jeffers's hair. Poe's hair
in a brooch "of spiral gold," you can see it coiled
tensely inside like a watchspring. Compton Mackenzie's
rubber toilet cushion and kilt. And "Clarence
E. Hemingway's first 3 white hairs." Earle Stanley Gardner's
brass knuckles and credit cards and his photographs
of 2 views of a skunk and his "Oriental bamboo sleeve gun
with blood-encrusted darts" and the tapes of him
learning Spanish. *This is all true.* And the hair, almost
always the hair, that most supremely voodooesque
of the body's various flotsam mnemonics we pick up
tangled and beached on an alien shore and with it recall
the whole life. Hair. A bottle village.
10,000 pencils, "you know." Iron mice.

———————

The candle's final stutter. And so
our last view of Hunt. He floats in front
of the bubbled, leaded window glass, an intermittent
orangeish flicker himself from the flame, like something
vaguely autumnal that's been pressed inside
these pages for preservation. Now he finishes
labeling Washington's packet—the birthdate,

31

1732. That year, Pope
is "engaged in building"—the garden, its nooks—
and planning his Grotto. The garden will have
a "triumphal arch," "shell temple," and
"a hot-house for ananas." (Foreign
blossoming is all the rage.) In 1734, the year
Pope sketches, for a friend, advisory plans
toward garden ornamentation, Collinson is down
at the London docks, is on his knees like Midas
pouring through a treasure chest, at this initial
of Bartram's shipments, *arrowwood, staggerbush,*
hellebore, alder, honeysuckle, lady's slippers...

———

The storm is a lulu. A ringtailed king 'coon lulu
of a boulder-whomper. He ties a rag of the rat-bag
over the horse's jittery eyes, and in that band of relative
calm, the horse calms. Bartram, though, is excited
past containment. Every atom of the air's seems individually
rinsed and charged. A little ways over, the hills look
like the First Day out of Genesis; and he firms up the knot
in the horse's tether, once more pats her slobbery muzzle,
then walks out from under their overhang, into
rain like scrapers at work on old paint. The hell
with the lightning. He's getting old, he hasn't that
many more gathering-trips left in him, and this is
his adopted atavistic family out there, tree
and bird and lizard, and he's going to lie on the crown,
the nipple, the wizard's-cap tip, of that highest hill
and sing in celebration of the creatures of Creation.
John Bartram. "A very proper person to gather seeds."

In his writings, he played with strange ideas that Egyptians
or Carthaginians had landed once in America,
and he surmised some land bridge linking his country to China.
What he knew best of China was one impressive half-handfull
of aster seeds, from the Jesuits there to France
and then to London, when Collinson thought to ship them over
as a gift to his backwoods procurer. What Bartram
thought exactly of all that Chinese land mass spinning in a night
that was forever our day, I don't know, if he dreamed

the flora of Mars and the Moon, if he itched to trade shoots
with a gardener of the Khan's, if the call of the stars was
drowned (or wasn't) by the nearer clamor
of anthers, rattlers, bee buzz, sap and bud... He
said of the cosmos, "Orbs beyond orbs, without number,
suns beyond suns, systems beyond systems, how
can we look on these without amazement!" Because
he said it, a man on a hill in a storm, with his back
on the rain-splattered grasses of North Carolina and
his face to the sky, I think of him

on my own night walks with the fire of wanting
down to the seedgerm and up to the stars
alive in me and leaping. I have
a woman I love, and the 1921 *Poetry* (October) with Stevens's
strict and flinchless "The Snow Man" inside, and it's
never enough. In the days of desire, impossible
numismatic lust for the coins off the eyes of the great dead
fills our nerve-ends. Something that may be coins gives the face
on the shroud of Turin an open gaze, I
want them, give me the sinewy vault
of Shelley's heart, the spiral filaments of wood that twisted
delicately at the last from Paul Revere's devoted whittling
of Washington's false teeth, let me have the names of every
flaming body on the star chart
that's tattooed to be the pattern of our retinal plates
as surely as nubile hula girls and burning skulls are tattooed
on the biceps of half the drunk bikers in World's End,
Oklahoma, let me know who cares to carry it on
and start an album off with a curl of Leigh Hunt's, and
hand me just one sketch of a plant that Bartram did,
or one leaf of the sketch, or a single green vein
where he lavished exactment and wonder... The storm

is over by now. He's drained—as if his taking in so
much of the world is reciprocal this once, and the world
has absorbed him. The clouds thin. The first stars faintly
come forward. He thinks the band of night has arrived
here at last from China, and now it will calm things
like the rag around his horse's eyes, and then it will pass on
schedule back to the Orient, and then return... And so he sees,

John Bartram, who "cast my eyes on a daisy
with more curiosity than common country farmers are wont,"
he sees his Earth is one more night-striped weather-marbled
sphere of a collection, countless, spinning in the ineffable ordering
system of the heavens. The moon shows up by now as a true
blood orange fully come to ripeness, and a man on a hill
is howling for it. Or not the moon exactly, but some
idea of time and how to use it. And not exactly
a howl. At speed and with details both
too immense to imagine, the planet turns over and
over and somewhere a man is always making a salvager's small
high sounds of wanting.

This is what you know, John Bartram,
isn't it: every day the whole planet turns upside-down

without disrupting our passions

———

a hairsbreadth.

Some Art

The Elements

The cool, dusk-blue of the shadows of these Dutch plums
is mixed with a quarter-thimble of gray that matches
   glints in the skins of the pears, the berries, the liver-paste.
If the dull swell of a herring on a plate picks up
   red chevrons meaning a candle (out of sight) is lit,
the crystal of burgundy weighting another corner is given
   a small red heart of light at its center so
everything, in shape and weight, is balanced, and
   the keen lines angled like stylized rain around
the base of the creamer say the same green as the stems
   that have been set like accent-marks for the scansion of cherries.
In the back, in the middle, a hot loaf is broken
   for steam to rise in a perfect column of nearly
corinthian detail, at the edges of which it thins
   in equilibrium with the night, as a breath might
leave a body and settle, composed and ubiquitous.
   I wonder if this still-life exists in the universe

*

of a wormy handfull of rice. I wonder what the sense of time
   in which it was painted has to do with a year
in the dog cages. When a prisoner's released
   from one of those, he "walks" by sitting, moving his legs
ahead of him by hand, like huge quaint compasses.
   This group was abducted out of their homes and now will be kept
at an "interim camp." They face the camera with something
   in their eyes beyond despair. Before the film goes
to a New York-based reporter summing it up, we see
   a newly-uncaged woman catch a doll
a soldier tosses her, then start to comb its patchy hair, and only
   hours later will we come to understand this
is her infant daughter dead of cold water and lye.
   I wonder, in all of science-fiction, if there have been
two universes this discordant, or what it means
   that there can be a suffering so intense its balance only
exists somewhere in the next life. And

*

I wonder if I should hate that painting, I wonder
if out of faith kept with the brutalized, I should revile
    the easy leisure with which another world applied its dedication
to a study of shadow lengthening under tangerines, I
    wonder if now we must love that painting more than ever,
its calm, its idea of order and abidingness, I wonder
    isn't this exactly the freedom for which we risk the cage
and dream of in the cage to keep us living, this
    aloof, light space in which the heft of a peach against
washed linen can grow important and exact,
    I wonder if I should burn a painting like that
and turn to the knife and the placard, I wonder if
    I should give my days to the completion of its housing
under temperature control, I wonder what we give
    our nights to, and how much our days define our nights, I
wonder until I sleep, and I sleep like a fresh bread
    cooling, reaching an agreement with the elements.

"The Numbering at Bethlehem"

He was, he tells his grandson, a grandson
himself. He'd got a red-and-white bone fish hook with his
name on, inscribed by a peddler who knew such things, and he was
fishing "chust like ve are now, troo a liddle hole in d'ice" but
then a catfish big about as a soldier's boot
with whiskers like broomstraws, gulped bait
hook and all and waggled clean away. Another time... The
boy's not listening. He's lost inside
the coalseam streaks in the living fillet of a half-gutted perch
in their basket. It's cold, tomorrow may be colder. His breath
is small and white and leaves his body not unlike, he
thinks, evisceration. His body is small. His whole vignette
—the creel mother weaved, the two poles propped and crossed
like sloppy heraldry, his grandfather muttering
history and dribble—is small in Breughel's
composition of rhythmic smallnesses.
                              If the title is Biblical,
still this is a 16th-century Flemish village and all
its huff and clutter is true to the shape of that
specific time and place.
An innkeep's offals-boy is sawing his knife
through the deepest hoses and breads
in the throat of a hog; it's stunned and even
so, he needs to keep one knee in its ribs; obligingly,
a serving-girl is here with her long-handled pan for the branch
of blood jutting out. They hear the carpenters Breughel's
lifted dimly into farther ground (this winter
air will carry sound with the thwang of a metal bannister).
There are four, applied to a framework. It's a function
of how far they are that stylization makes them smooth black
silhouettes of tools themselves: an adze, a hatchet.
One arm of the Y-support is sleeved in snow so rich it
seems less fallen from the sky, and more to have risen
like cream from the common white on the ground. Deliverers
drag an ice-sledge over the lake. Two girls, with sticks, propel
themselves on dining platters. Others have skates. Three chickens
pecking snow could be a homily on faith in a providence
greater than winter's thinness, if anyone noticed.
Nobody notices.

Nearly 200 figures, and nobody sees
what we see, in administrative
overview: receding wheels
lead the eye discursively into perspective: cart ones,
wagon ones, loose ones left to whiten in ice like ghosts
of wheels, wheels as tall as a man and dwindling
with the men as plane gives way to plane, down distance.
So they make a wreath,
three barrel mouths, and a scatter of baskets
units of a pattern. Nobody notices,
either, the woman on a donkey—just a bent head really,
tented in a voluminous cloak of blue. Why
should they? Everybody has his own white
bellows of breath to contend with.
                              "Und voomen—
you tink your Grandpapa is so old alvays he nefer
made sniksnak vit voomen?" By the shine in his eye
you'd think that here was salty revelation to make
the white breath of its telling shine, like a new-used ivory
prosthetic in a seraglio. Maybe it does. But the boy's still
worlds away, is living now in a contemplation of bubbles
on the underside of the thinnest ice, like winter grapes
in a rice-white bunch. In a way it's a pity. His grandfather's
breaths, like anyone's, are nothing so much as a true cast
of the insides of a man; to the extent that this implies the oldest
wholeness of the family is on display, it is. It
disappears, though, unattended, in the air. "Yah, two
goot vives here, hah, but den I go fight, you know?, for kings
in lants so far avay. Vhen I return..."
And soforth. We don't see it either, really. This man
and his grandson are an inch or two outside
the frame of the painting, and whatever half-mile or so of
pewter-, delft- and lime-green lake-ice that this means.
We see, immediately
                              and instead, what almost everybody
sees and clusters hotly about, if not
by curiosity then by proclamation: census-takers,
one in a nearly-regal coat of fox and weasel, number
this village (the reference is to Bethlehem,
of course, and so their particular,
secret interest is in Jews, just,
or about to be, born). This off-center
hub of the general turning of action is in the near left corner,

saying its early New Testament story in loud
concentration of earth-reds. Wasn't that the text
the priest read every year around Christmas?: Herod,
Judas, Calvary, redemption... What was it he said... Perhaps
the few, far, detail-less churchgoers
will know in a moment, stamping loaves of old snow
off their leggings, then assembling themselves
like sacks of goods on the long hard pews. To them,
we assume, this isn't the horizontal level of least detail
at all: somebody's stubble picks up purpled light
through the stained glass wound of a martyr, so looks
like velvet nap; a baby's drool, by virtue
of that same slash and its pouring, is a mother's loveliest
jewel as it rests in a clutter of cheap brass trinkets;
someone's hoe left in the anteroom, someone's stoatskin mittens...
So another time, with its network of information, is in
the lineaments of this ordinary day in 1566, a few nights'
ride from Brussels. And if that's distractive
referential layering
for us, no wonder no one plaiting osiers for the seat
of a much rewickered backyard bench, or piling handwidth brick
on brick in a hod, or shooing a dramatic captain of rats
from its exploratory swagger through the bagged beets,
sees
          the man who leads the donkey from another story
into this one, is hungry
and his woman in the blue cloak seems to be holding herself
as if she, too, were a tent,
a tent of flesh, and an ember inside is keeping her
warm despite the weather. For that matter,
no one sees the way the rounded banks of snow are hard-edged
crystal adhering to crystal, over and over, until they gently
blend; or how the snow is paint
that's snow; or how the dough-white fresh-washed puffy cap
of the serving-girl holding the blood-pan is an agency by
which the mounds of snow in their lateral vanishing
are repeated, here, in smaller but
similar form. "...Vhen I return, yes?, I go
fishing, chust like dis." What was it he said? Yes,
let's just rest and fish now, not try so demandingly
hard to see. "Und you know vhat I catch? Dis is, oh,
yah, so many years later." Let's just sit and listen
lazily,

      these few blue allegorical December days
B.C. What was it he said
about our lives? *They fit* About our deaths?
into a grand design. As a boy,
you believed it. One boy's
back in the thick of his grandfather's story again. "Some
damn pretty fish
wit' my hook, wit' my red-and-white bone hook in his botty!"
They fit into a grand design.

U

Very young children, even the newborn, have special abilities which they
spontaneously seem to forget in middle childhood and have to "relearn" as they
grow older. This behavior is termed U-shaped.

In 1900, a deep-frozen carcass of a woolly mammoth was discovered in the
permafrost of the Siberian arctic... Since then, many more of the preserved beasts
have been found.

—from two entries in *The World Almanac*
Book of the Strange #2

This convoluted brain-gray paint is haze, on paint
some follower of Turner intends as water. A chalky,
crushed-mulberry gray in the middle distance darkens
at its center to what might be a man out rowing, but
approaching or receding we can't tell. And so he's
both, as in those optical illusions where the construct pulses
toward us then away. That's all we know. The rest we need
inventing: earlier, he gathered a bouquet along the bank
(and so reflects the one I bought at the florist's) and
now, in this fog, it's a torch-orange smudge in the boat-bottom.
Then the onset and completion of his journey, that we read
in alternation, say some hesitancy in the when and the why of the
giving of those flowers (so reflect my own). And where
he'll be / he has been, when the haze obscures him, ah,

is a story only the woolly mammoth could tell, of being
in the deep gray of a holding place so far, so faithfully
ministering to the forms of its figures, it means another
world exists. That's all we know. The rest we need inventing:
he reaches the open sea; or he lands at a shack where a second and
diversionary woman offers easy, immediate pleasures;
or he enters an order of holy brothers vowed to silence, and
now the breath in sleep, the scrape of fork on china,
come to be the music for his prayers... Let's say
in that world, gray has opened up to morning like the throat
of a furnace, tigerish, tulip-crimson, fuming.
He's bent at a desk. He's writing, a poem, by the shutters.
The gold light falls like insignia-stripes on his paper, and
fog and rowing aren't part of him now. Memory

does this—stitches in and out. The way she tilts
her face in tenderness (the whole day realigning
every leaf and bend of sewerpipe to her angle)
drops entirely from your neural record, lets a life go on,
a house, the shadows of a street, the little daily
eruptions of lust and money, what we call dreaming,
what we call the cold slap of being awake... and then one
day reappears, from nowhere, from another world: her
face; and you can feel every star adjust position. So
a man might be returning, through the haze, with something
for her. A dozen, bright and damp. And I forgot
to say one woolly mammoth was found with the buttercups
still in a group on its tongue, perfect, an offering out of the gray.
A long turn for a bouquet to take. *Here.*

Poem Whose Last Sentence Is 17 Syllables
After a Suggestion

The little we need. Thoreau demoted flour in favor of lowlier
Indian meal *which the farmer will offer his hogs,* but he
baked savorily enough in a pit-fire, yeastless and
utter, this final plank of bread his food reduced to.
So: another night with woodsmoke and *The Odyssey* being
sufficience along his pond's sweet weed-hipped shore. The

little we need, we *need.* And for me it's down, these days,
to a soapstone rabbit, so slick even light slips off
its globous haunches' skin; a quiet Steinberg print
(the still-life items held in a consensus of pastels); and
the carton for **DR. STRONG'S BLOOD PURIFIER** "heals
Man or Beast," its bottle (I'm sorry) long gone. —Far cry

from the minimal whisper at Walden, I know; but
what can I say? Some deepening afternoons, the shadows
of lamp posts falling across the streets make a gauntlet;
each next one is a heavier blow in a day of heaviness,
yes, and I cringe home to where these objects say,
however they do and whatever the reason, some version of

serenity. So: friends most opposed to ownership still
own talismanic knickknacks. At her handlopped-beam and adobe
home in the sand stone steerskull gully land of New Mexico,
that she bought for ten dollars, O'Keeffe shows her bedroom:
the bed, one plain straight chair, a wedge of fireplace.
"This is my corner," she says. "I haven't anything

you can't get along without." And so the one
adornment startles: the hand of a Buddha statue, straightup
in "The *mudra* That Banishes Fear." Dark hand fixed high
on a dull buff wall, it seems the Buddha is parting
the veil between our world and his plane of
fire tigers and Absolute Composure—in a moment he'll

45

step full-bodied in. O'Keeffe is 94; maybe she *can't*
"get along without" his Banishing Fear. Night's indigo
mysteries seep through, and the hand is a great calm, and
an easiness. Here, in my room, I look at 3 objects,
I'm the curator for 3 objects. They make something
of the way the center of wood accepts pressure. Sometimes

reading filler on the whizz!bang! megabuck microchip
dreck-stuffs smugly cached in cornerstones for the future's
drooling of oohs, I think a solid block of mahogany more
the ideal time capsule. They mean that to me.
3 objects. It works like this: by night, some nights,
the lamp posts' shadows sink compacted in my body,

deeply: striated muscle. The world's worked
worry, busyness and its hooplah gratuitous feedbacks,
finally, that far into my fibers. There's much
too much. Even my own residue-accumulating
daydreams. Even these detailed superexempletive stanzas
you're reading. —When something... the hand of the Buddha

breaks into the poem /right here/ and a voice says
Simplify, and cherish. One haiku. Three objects.
Outside, the ribs of one bananatree leaf
individuate late spring breeze. At the end of an arm
of moonlight, DR. STRONG will heal me, "guaranteed."
It's my Indian meal—one cupworth. It's "a restorative,"

it says—yes, it says it's a restorative.

Paolo Uccello

*...would spend the whole night at his drawing-
board working to find the rules of perspective, and
when his wife tried calling him to bed, he would call
back, "Oh, how sweet is this perspective!"*
                                                    —Vasari's *Lives*

It's not so much an argument is taking place—the argument *becomes*
the place, takes over: and their arbor-tenders' plaited straw hut is
filled like a mold, by invective and defensiveness. He's
right, she is a maggot-riddled lemon-puss. And she's right, it's
in urgent, earned response to his abusive fists. They're both
right, that the other's wrong; the luscious citrus sun of the Medicis
sets, and each sleeps in a corner so emotionally cold they could be
Ant- and Arctic polar caps—though we don't know the world is round,

in Florence, in 1456. And even so... It's night, and
by his oil's buttery puddle of light, Paolo Uccello, 2 generations
in front of Columbus, is venturing to the horizon.
Whistling. Lost in it. Making his paint go
dozens of green miles deep. Sleep floats the bickering couple
over their grapes... the palace sentry nods... the tavern whore
hics into a doze... But here in the clutter-dumped workshop
in the Piazza San Giovanni, *The Battle of San Romano*

———

rears and charges and blows the lathery snot of excitement
out of its manifold nostrils. Where the Florentine and Sienese
forces' horses clash, their trappings clink in one unbroken
golden flow across the right-hand foreground. Every leaf
is veined. Each blossom lifts its petals for inspection.
Trees bear oranges as substantial as pawnshop balls.
The armor, hinged; the bridles, incised; the broken lances mouth
their splintered grain; and everything says *here*. There,

though—and lovely—in the upper third, in the terra-verde
fields of receding, detail fades. It's far. The hedges,
smooth; the soldiers' faces, small denominations of faces.
This is Paolo Uccello's passion. These are the endlessly long
green stems for which the battle is only the gaudy bouquet.
And where the stems converge... Whistling. Lost in it.

47

So far, now the stems are threads. He's taking them back
to the knot, the node, the navel, behind the picture plane. And in back

———

of a painting of battle is a battle: real, bone juts out
from shredding flesh and the faces of the dead are blue and rot.
In back of that there will always be stories. In this one,
a man named Bendetti, a Florentine, betrayed his city.
One night under the umber roofs he sold some information and
the next day troops were ambushed. This is only one
of the stories lined up behind any story, like Paolo Uccello's
distance-system of grids. For instance, in World War II

a man named Avrom Murmel betrayed the Jews of his ghetto,
in Molnsk, in occupied Poland. This was what they called
The Unspeakable Days. 12 people slept in a room; there were no sewers,
which was good: that winter they burned their shit. A shift
was 14 hours: so many bundles, a cup of soup; no bundles,
no soup—and most of the childrens' ribs pushed out like rakes.
The Gangs even took some children, and some of the old
—to "rest farms." Maybe. This is where Murmel comes in,

———

around the time the sacks of bone meal start appearing. And so
an effort was made to hide the young, the old, "the fertilizer ones"
—so street talk had it. Murmel sold their location. Maybe
they would have been found out anyway. Probably; who knows?
He did this a few times. Once, at a rumor of riot, the Gangs
threw something into a crowd: a 6-month-old
with a lit stick of dynamite shoved through its anus. This
became a symbol for Murmel's collaboration. And he, of

course, refuted any connection between that ghastliness and
his pay. As for the "rest farms," they were likely real; go
ahead, prove otherwise. The hidden Jews would have been discovered
other ways, surely—and then with drastic repercussions his
intervention precluded. Besides, a handfull here or there, but hundreds
of healthy adult workers were saved that way—he, Murmel,
saved them! You live, you have your own wife and child to think of,
things hurt you but you try your best. Anyway, that was his perspective.

48

A Book About Rembrandt

The human pineal is a small endocrine gland, about the size of a mustard seed;
it has evolved, or devolved, from the "third eye" common to many lizards and
fish and so, while lying deep in the brain, is still presumably sensitive to light.

And then—for the siege had long before depleted their foods—
they bundled the children in what protective amuletic stuffs
might seem to ask the dead's forgiveness, and under the heavy
dovegray moon-refuting clouds of that season, one night
entered the cemetery and ate the grass and ivy off
the graves. It was done in a perfect, stupid,
herbivore's silence; no one whimpered, no one joked.
At least that's the story his mother told him. Now
she's underground too. The stories she told and the story
she's become are closed, and Rembrandt is lost

———

in a problem of mass and light that only exist, and
tremblingly, in a continuous present. He's working
a dray cart teasingly out of a bank of smoky bister,
and the horse's head is a gray sack with its contents going
slowly bad, the sky is gray, the ground is grayish-brown,
but somehow the fruits on the cart are washed in a specific
light so pearly, they glisten as if with alchemical droplets,
transfiguring, immanent. Blurried background shapes are
small—as small as his childhood is against this demanding
immediacy, its oils and rags... when I close the book

———

on Rembrandt, for this view a tilt of wing admits fired and
fine-grained through my airplane window. Rivers are runs
of fresh glass still with the furnace-dazzle on them.
Sun gives hundreds of cars in a lot the fitted lapidaried
glint of links in a Tut-tiered necklace. Everything burns
itself for attention. Though it's easy enough to slide
my window closed and the world is a story I'm already
half-forgetting. So all the windows are closed, and light
is known now by this airplane as it must be to a sleeper:
only the pineal seed, in *its* deep crease, keeping photofaithful.

Dürer

*His natural fidelity and honesty caused him to
approach reality direct.*
                              —Marcel Brion

The dessicated flukes of a whale. A leech so
green it's black, and is the jewel being worn by a long
pink finger of pig meat. Below that,
twelve chanterelles. One is sliced in half, so is the window
to a sunset on a ridge with one unbreakable pine, all
done from the color of mushroom, by a mushroom, in a mushroom.
A roc's egg. A geode. A walrus tusk. The planisphere
of cherrywood and cedar, with a fistfull of planets
of particolour Venetian glass, and token stars like anthers
on fine wire stalks—nearby, the ornate ivory key
for its employment. Fox-fur robes. The shell of an ocean crab
as wide as a child's face. A length of linen, hard and
modeled into difficult garnet twists by someone's
month-blood; it had been around and in her for a day.
A suit of armour. Beside it, the detailed, dour
sketch of a rhinoceros. A vast green lace of seaweed
over the mantle, and a bagpipes like the hellish genitalia
of some creature from the sea. A jar of brine.
Inside it, the rough nub of a fifth leg
from a stillborn sheep. A linnet's wing. A radish
in the shape of a couple rammed headlong in sex.
A radish in the shape of Christ on the Hill
with even the nails in depiction. A slice of
cat placenta, in lemon juice in a bright blue plate.
A knucklebone. A ferret's skull.
An oar. A horn inkwell. An owl's claw.
Is this what he needed to study, to draw
the clear, true, crosshatched portrait or self-portrait of a man?
This is what he needed to study, to draw
the clear, true, crosshatched portrait or self-portrait of a man.

A Window Seat

...how carefully the Renaissance masters designed up.to the limit of the frame, the rectangle being accepted and emphasized in the design. The Baroque painters, on the other hand, endeavor to suggest or even to force upon the spectator, the supposed continuation of the imagined picture space beyond and behind the frame...
"TAKE ME!"

...At which time I close my Roger Fry, successfully
seduced by an in-flight movie. I know it, or
of it from reviews: this actress flung in a sexy x
on the bed, her peignoir making smoky open wings,
died 5 days into production. Everybody talking to her
talks to empty air she's later spliced, lithe, lusciously,
into. When an actor lusts for her, she's someone out
of the world of this room he's in, and out of the room

of this world now completely. Below, while I fly
to a string of small-town readings, my wife is marking
her sister's early death's first anniversary, at the side
of the freshly flowered-over grave in Waco. I know she'll be
speaking, softly and with an intimate, strict attention,
as if Emily were just beyond some pane of light too
blinding for sight's going through, though with the easy motes of
this life's constant motion in it, and permeable. Words

of simple catching-up—this has happened, that—to someone so
far into the shine of mica, the scales of weathering, time
outdistances news. I eke my slide-up panel open and
"below" becomes the lovely abstract cataracting greens
and sorghum-reds of cultivation—now Pollock, now
Mondrian—or the sharp, if doll-sized, blueprints of communities
long-buried but clear from the air as rows of post-pits,
darker ditch-grass, chalky discs. The Nazca

lines in south Peru cross miles of dun-tone desert, make enormous
geometry-wingéd birds, fish, even a monkey, for the high eye
of a jetliner or a god, for that eye only (Pan-American highway
workers bulldozed smackdab through those shapes and
never saw them). A hummingbird 100 yards requires that
distance the way this actress—also slight in "real life" but
larger as an image, peignoir tremblingly, exotically (almost
congruently with the bird) spread wide—requires

51

time outside her time, before we see her acting
interacting with the living cast. So Morgan will set her few
considered flowers down, and simply say "I've missed
you, Em." She'll weep a little. Of course—her sister a figure
that's reached the vanishing point. But that's the point
exactly where matters of faith take over from matters of paint
—and Morgan's eyes will blur, and Emily speak back,
genuine, tender. So it is that there's a universe outside this

poem this poem's aware of, flush against it, crowded and
extraneous: Squid are folded over a clothesline. Cops
are staking out Le Go Go where the mastectomized dancer is
storing the coke in her foam breast. Someone's dissertation is so
many aphids pushing up so much nutritional goop, per day, per colony.
From a back pew, someone sees the plaster Christ let real blood
and writhe. The perfect planetarium is the night sky
under a goose's wing: small dependable domed dark. All

that, and more, while in this poem (and out of it) I
slide my groundview closed; return half-dozing to the gravity
of movieland body for body; fidget; land—it's no
flat study now but people, wheels, meals, deals, dimensional and
rubbing at the skin. In my motel tonight, from
this height, open beardtrim scissors leave a pterodactyl
fossil in damp and rust on the sink. Some light has come
from the moon to fall on the Roger Fry. The book,

the window, have me thinking Vermeer: inevitably
his picture is a room, the room is filled with the spilling
of thick Delft light through a window, giving pewter that special
white richness of milk, and cloth the depth of landscape,
light from somewhere unknowable glowing off the simple
frames the maps are in, the mirrors, the family portraits.
Soon I'll phone and Morgan say Emily said
she's ok, disembodied now (to us), at home on her own plane.

Knees / Dura-Europos

—to Judy

1. 255 A.D.

This is what's happening now: it's raining, mean
thick arrows of rain, on the swollen,
purple Euphrates side of the Roman garrison town
Europos, and a thinner, bitter, blue-gray taste of it
billows in, over the workers. Soon they're drenched.
They keep on anyway. Not that the sun would be kinder.
The siege is expected soon—the horsecuntsucking
Sassanians, coming out of the west, the desert, and so
the whole walled western frontside of this
fleablown frontier post is being filled with a buffer
of rubble. It'll be watery pig's-ass soup and endless
crotch-itch once the siege begins, and little
better now: the commander, the trundles of rock,
the rain starting in like a cat-o'-nines. And now this
crazy Jew in the downpour, running around them in circles,
wailing with each pick swung at his synagogue's stones.

*

This is what's happened before: on the site
of their old house of worship, the Jews of Europos,
tolerated benignly under this Roman regime, have had
constructed the current tile-ceilinged, wall-bemural'ed
House of the Glory of God. There isn't a one who didn't
shoulder brick—and tithe, or more, his hidden saving's-pinch
for this. The "this" is simple, and in its simplicity
lovely: the 4 walls have been painted completely
in warm-tone tempera—rose, sienna,
butter, blush, rich garnet, plum, buff, saffron—
and the depth of color substitutes
emotional repletion for perspective, in these flat
rough workings-out of the Bible. Jacob
dreaming angels. An Egyptian princess, shamelessly,
nakedly, umber-deepened pink, retrieving
Moses from the Nile. Ezra reading the law.
Esther saving her people. The building *is*

a picture Bible. —The spirit of which might best be
here, in The Binding of Isaac, done in a few
clear lines against a cerulean blue
above the Torah shrine itself. The boy is a scroll-like long,
limp bundle on his altar. The ram is already
come out of its thicket—really one
shrubby tree. And awestruck, with his back to us,
facing the bound boy, Abraham stands with his knife
upraised and sees the Hand of the Maker-of-All float
low in the heavens, human-shaped but huge, with the signal
desist. It's the Hand
of a strict, but compassionate, Maker-of-All.
With a little courage, and Jacob's ladder, a man
might climb to shake it.

*

This is what's happening now: a man is running
in circles, around the bottom-rung Roman soldiers
on wall-fill detail. Shmú-el ben Yedaya,
the *Cohen* (priest), is running wailing around the synagogue,
his synagogue and his people's, past
the colonnaded forecourt, around the study rooms
and back, in the rain, to the jeers of the crew,
is running a little crazed, is running knowing
this destruction is inevitable and to the common good,
this wedge- and batteringlog-destruction
of his synagogue and his people's, and though this is long
before the invention of anything truly a watch, he's running
in circles as if time might be wound
this way, now that it's running down, and by
his circles he might start it
at the beginning again.

*

And this is what's going to happen: the Sassanians
will arrive, and be successful. The Jews,
like everyone else, will either be slaughtered
or taken for slaves. The lucky will simply be
cut down, maybe raped and then cut down,
maybe forced to see a daughter raped and then
cut down, but anyway quickly. Others will be
unlucky, made to play with their own unraveled
bowels first, made to climb the pole and sit
with anus centered on its sharpened tip while
weights are piled on... And it's the same Hand,
of the same attentive Maker, that will allow all
this.

2. 1982–83

When Emily died—my sister-in-law, at 34,
of her lungs filling up with the self-drowning watery mucilage
of cystic fibrosis, all night under the respirator and finally it
just tore through the delicate cell-wall of her breathing...
It was bad. For months my wife held conversations
with her in sleep. "And when she was dead I
combed her hair a last time." Who all her life was brave
in her array of apparatus, and worked in the ward with the children
first having that nightmarish rubbery stuff pulled
out of their lungs. And every day the paper says some
goon politico celebrated his 90th birthday with high-fly whores
on either arm and a platinum magnum of rum. On the night
of condolences, I needed to run. My leg (again) was bum
and the rains had started, but this was an hour of working
everything out, in tens of thousands of sour pore-sized quanta,
that I needed—so I left the house of formal black,
in running shoes, and gave myself to the zigzag macadam trails
of Richardson, Texas. Now whenever I run
in rain, or with that deep complaining returned to my knee,
I always spend some terrible,
mnemonic minutes running through Richardson, Texas
—in Iowa, even, in St. Louis.
                              Grief
is never lonely. Any grief is every grief all
over again. Is any aching bone
joined unto bone joined unto bone in you and
out of you, down all the bones, till all the buried make one
smooth-joindered skeleton of which you're just the most recently
fleshed appendage. Morrie who
hugged his own chest, once, like a mother her dying child.
And then did die, his chest having stopped.
Sylvia's grandmother. Leslie my student a package
of leukemia. She was only 19. She wrote sweet unaccomplished
verses about "tinkling brooks." And no prayer,
imprecation or vial of Holy Water brought back taped
to a gilt-edged card with the story of Lourdes in calligraphy
stops it, ever. I'm a man in Austin,
jogging tonight, and the city is wet in the same
allotment of rain that drenched Europos once, that's been
our share bounced back between the Earth and Sky from long

before the Romans, long before the geese
in the mud of Imperial Rome—before the mud itself.
A night like this, a man can see the cycle of vapor
and cloud-completion taking place as if in giant textbook arrows,
making a great,
relentless wheel, large enough for the grinding
of all those bones.
                    I jog through the neighborhood park
—and the floral darkness, cleaned by the rains
like black glass freshly squeegeed, tells me: History
is only Time's way of washing itself,
of putting on new lemon scent
each spring and starting over.
                    I jog by the corner
downtown where the hookers are out in laminated makeup
even this weather can't smear, are out there
pacing like carousel horses in lurid lavender manes
—they tell me: History is a whore's life
told to 20 johns a night. She lies and no
two of them get the same story. Although the basic
bonework's always there: some good times,
then pain, then abandonment.

                              *

It was Dura first, an Assyrian name, at its founding.
When it fell to the Seleucids in 323 BC, they
named it: Europos.
Then it fell to the Parthians: Dura.
Then the Roman emperor Trajan took, and
successive Roman rule renamed, it: Europos.
Then the Sassanians won it: Dura. Archeologists
simply call it Dura-Europos, to avoid confusion.
No wonder, though, a man is confused.
No wonder a man runs circles. In 1921
the British and Arabs are fighting in the desert.
When the British dig trenches in preparation for Arab attack,
they come upon ruins... "The Sassanians
occupied Dura-Europos for only a brief time, very
soon abandoning it to the elements."
Crazy, running, wailing as he runs.

                              *

57

The Earth says: vapor.
The Sky says: rain.
There isn't any wisdom from this.
And if pain has a use, it's as part of the
cycle of pain. Like any self-contained system,
it feeds on, and leads to,
perpetual self.

3. Anytime

Listen: another story of during a war—so faceless,
so accurate in its hyperbolic approximations of daily life,
it could be any time or place or people.
                                        They
found their synagogue destroyed, and what the arson hadn't
damaged the axes and mallets did. (And a baby girl
had been trapped in back; on her, the fire
fed itself so greedily, they couldn't tell if here too the
mallets had been at work.) The heart of a whole
community, in pieces. And reconstructing it would mean fire
again, axes again, the police at the door past midnight.
So: you give up, right? Let someone else go worship
Yahweh-Who-Let-This-Happen. Right? Right
horseshit. Here's what you do:
                                        You go to work,
you come home in the purple thick of evening, you eat,
you go visit friends. And each of you brings a flute,
a flute for a little stupid peasant after-dinner music,
                  a bone flute.
It takes seven of those for her body to be
refastened as a menorah. And by
its light each night, abbreviated, silent, while
a few of you tootle on cheap tin flutes divertingly
near the windows, service
still ascends past the witnessing roofs of this city
as it has for generations.
                                        This
took planning. Resumption always takes planning,
argument, a graph. Though first it takes a while
of mournful circles, confused and cathartic,
run in the moment's version of pummeling rain, around,
around, before
the springwork mechanism of time is wound back ready
for setting again to the proper, ongoing tick. You've
felt him in you, haven't you?—Shmú-el ben Yedaya,
rounding your heart's bruised corners, maybe
for something so small as the getting
up to face a day. Then

59

you got up. When Jennie Burns
his wife of 17 years was lost to cardiac failure, Burns spent
12 months grieving; 12 more mothering each measured beat of
his sensitized own: walked soft, moved slow, in bed by 8,
until the doctor said his care was killing him, prescribing
go out and get laid. If he's circling this
hookers' corner with each fist on the wheel a little crazy, I
wish him, finally, a resurrectory night; I wish
the spirit of Jennie be calm and forgiving, out there in the overgoverning
circuitry of pi-mesons and suns.
                              Listen: late in the 19th century, maybe
into the 20th, mummies from the digs and market hucksters
grew so numerous, railroads used them instead of coal. Whole
family burial plots were fed to the locomotives. Now the standard
response is supposed to be oh, what a loss to science or oh,
the sacrilege. Yes, there's that; the sacrilege.
                              But
stand on the edge of the desert in that brief retrieving
season when the fires die down and a small cloud hints
a whole sweet, green, revivifying sky is on its way.
One day we'll curse the rain, its chill, the yellow phlegm.
One day we'll curse the sun's ordained return. But
every year we stand here, thrilled, our skin so
open and hopeful, as a man might stand in one
of a million Duras, and with that rising
piquant breeze from out of the long, fierce, leafless
wastes
            we understand: that the dead must be used
to power the living.
                        That sounds a little grand. And
when I run, it's such a trivial
circle traced on the face of it all. Another taking
up of an hour. Another guy out, working it off. But
still, it's a circle. And Shmú-el ben Yedaya must be
one more orbit, must be necessary according to the most
primordial formula, must be one more added balance
here, where we live, on our level between
the revolutions of subatomic particles and the
system-spin of stars. Come on:
I'm tying my shoes. Come on already,

60

                                        I'm jogging
through the blind moon's white cane tapping about
a lush black stand of liveoak, past the laundromat's blather
of hum and slosh, around the pond, by the caryard,
to hell with the pinch when the leg bends wrong, come on.
I don't know what fake name the whore gave Burns
or what her story was this thousandth time with some new yokel
curious and hesitant at the edge of the bed, but I know it
must have ended like anyone else's autobiography,
I'm here, and more often than not that's a version of triumph.
And I don't know the colloquial gripe-and-fuss-words someone mumbled
in revery, painting the synagogue plaster (now
the Red Sea's being split like a loaf of heavy, red bread)—that,
or the formal language with which he labeled
some of his simple figures standing in their simple
Biblical narratives of what travail
becomes. But I can give you a rough translation,
in the cut-and-dried no-nonsense one-line oratory
my doctor sometimes uses at the last when jargon seems to be beside
the point:
                The heart is more
important than the knees.

I'm keeping on jogging despite my pain.
I'm keeping on praying despite my God.

Some People

Wings

I always wondered why they called them wings.
—Perhaps because somebody always waited in shadow
in them, with a rope.
With a rope like a great braided nerve,
and while some sweet singing or bloody melee
completely filled the central light, this person
would raise or lower the god.

*

It's summer. Hard summer; the land enameled.
I find the bird already half-dismantled
by ants—the front half. It's flying
steadily into the other world, so needs to be this still.
Do I mumble? yes. Do I actually pray? yes.
Yes, but not for the bird. When we love enough
people a bird is a rehearsal.

The Poem of the Praises

Tho' always unmarried I have had six children.
—Walt Whitman

No plausible claimant has ever come forward.
—Justin Kaplan

My name isn't Lucius; I never grew up
to own the mill down at Spiritwood, where the falls makes the river a blue leg
slipping into the long white laces of a *danseuse*;
where the marl pit is, and the radiant amber and ember-red wildflowers
like powers, thrones and dominions putting on bearable form; I
never consolidated with Midas Mill Distribution, and contracted
later with Yancy Hobbs for the stream of half-price darkie sackers,
and later still negotiated the first use of the Edison illuminatory bulbs
in a 3-county area; and one day I didn't think of all the days,
and run into the meadow rubbing my face in the faces of flowers
like a rooting swine until someone came to speak carefully to me and carry
    me home.
   My name isn't Rebecca; I never bore three children,
of which Matthew died of the yellow phlegm while still at my nipple,
but Columbine is a poetess of renown and my sweet Lionel Alexander
is the governor's aide; I didn't enter Henry's study
while he was at cards, and open the book of that jackanapes rascal
Darwin as Henry referred to him, and finish the book, and form
my own opinions; I didn't color my conversation with these
while serving the tea, for years, a deep brown veritable
Ganges of tea, and its steamy, pervasive weather; I never
bled, at my "time"; I never crocheted; I never rode Heat Lightnin'.
   My name isn't Nathan Lee; I never gave up
seminary studies for astronomy—and that way traded heaven
for the sky; I never took as a lover the famous but stumbledrunk
opera tenor whose name I cannot here divulge, though he
and I like the stars were of the same mold and burning in affinity; and
at night in the observatory we never disported and wondered which
of the glass—the telescope lens leading high or the wine decanter going
increasingly low—could take a man farthest.
   My name isn't Patience; I wasn't a stillbirth; I
wasn't even a stillbirth.
   My name isn't Hamilton; and I was never ten; I never
gobbled grampa's Ladies Church League First Prize watermelon

entirely on the Fourth of July; and ran to the creek, to wash off; and
ran, I was as slick as a seed, and ran, past the burnt knoll, to the fields
where a mower whipped round at the charge of a wasp and his scythe
neatly severed my windpipe.

My name isn't Maysie; I wasn't released
at age 18 from the orphanage, to be a kerchiefed gypsy phrenologist
traveling with my monkey (Kip) and my body in bangles and taffeta,
a life of coins and kisses I would never trade to be a Queen; and
all the better for seeking out clues of my parentage, here
in a hedgerow, there in the chinese tea, wherever; I didn't find
my mother, a lovely colored woman the shade of a fawn's far underbelly,
of high rank in a Boston philanthropic society
dedicated to aiding her people, she had a room in a house
done up in sheaves of pressed African flowers and Mexican crucifixes,
and had that same excitement in her bones; I didn't find
my father, and who knows how many others' father, I didn't
approach an open window at dusk in that battlemarked slattern
of a house on Mickle Street, no; and if it happened, and
it didn't, I was 36 by then and he was ancient and ageless;
a candle was lit; he was writing; the hat he kept on was a crumpled
gray, the soft and shapeless gray of a dray-nag's muzzle,
his beard was that very color bleached by a shade; but the vase
was a fire of pinks and tiger lilies; he looked up from the page;
he didn't really see me, I could tell his eyes were still filled
with the page; and yet they said to me, *you are my child*; not
that it happened, it didn't; I left; a steady
current of people filled the street, alive and loud; his
eyes might have said it with just as much claim
to a hundred of them, in May, in Camden, New Jersey, in 1885.

And now we have read the books they write about our father,
singing his praises. This is the phrase they use: "singing his praises."
We, who never existed enough in his life, have read the singing
of the praises that never existed enough in his life, and now
from where we abide in the spaces between things touching, we
would like to sing his praises too. An antimatter chorus.
We would like to praise his words, they are so comely
in acceptance of the world with all of its rank perfume that sticks
in the creases and glazes over by morning, his words
that took the speech of horse-car conductors and walkup girls and
gave it the indigo-iridescent louse-ridden cosmos-connoitering
wings it deserves. We praise the ink of his words, it

is blacker and deeper than outer space though it fits in its
6-oz. crystal. And we praise the squid, that king
of all insomnia—whose ink glands mean perpetual night
is a living thing, tucked in its body. That king of diversion,
whose ink is a dummyself hanging credibly sized and shaped
in the waters—guardianangel-, golem-, doppelgänger-ink.
(And wasn't our father's ink his public being?) And
especially we praise the squid of the deep, we mean the *deep*,
where the waters are black and ink would be useless, but its
is a luminous cloud, a waft of bright light, a lamé.
(And wasn't our father's? Yes—wasn't our father's?) Now
a dozen squid are folded over a clothesline while the fishers finish
stacking their gear. We praise their knuckles a day's work's
rubbed dull garnet. We praise the air of the Greek islands over them
and in them, it has more dead than the air of some other places and
more honorable dead (we've seen our father open
Homer; marbled paper should be praised, and the raised
hubs of leatherbound spines). For every death filling the air, the lungs
have one accommodating alveólus, and this is efficient, fitting
synergy and cycling, so we praise the human body, every subatomic
pokerchip in the vast halls of its house rules. We
can never sing praises too many. Of even a rhizome, a protein,
one bulbette of roe. We have been waiting
in the null-spaces, here in the Byways of Possible Combination
one pi-meson wide, and we want to tell you those spaces are nothing
but genesis song. Sing with us. Simply be silent and
hear yourself sing. We are going to praise the almost-nothing
colors of malt and barley, in their barrels next to the dried green peas
and salt cod. We are going to sing for every string of sudden stiffening
below a nipple that flies it like a kite, for every wire
in a radio that's carried the news of murder in alternation
with the lyrics of love (doo-*wah*), for the life of the bottom-quark
(in trillionths of a second) and the life of the tortoise whose shell
time buffs to lustre its emerald burls over generations of men,
we're going to sing these praises and nothing can stop us, please
join in, we're going to sing of the perfect angle the beak of the
bluetit makes in territorial ardor, of the chipped hand
of a satyr on a bisque Pompeian vase, then of the chipped foot
of the maiden posed in flight, and how the signalman who's motioning
a jetliner into its bay is an eloquent stylized da Vinciesque figure
deserving of place in a pottery frieze for future archeological tweezers,
and of the moon, and of the nematode, and of the star-nosed mole,

and of the rumble of the moving van, and of the flash of a knife that
flashes other knives into the glare like one fish flicking
a whole silver school on its axis, and of a single scale in that school
distributing light's Newtonian range, of spare change
jiving in a pocket like an *a cappella* group in a basement club, the notes
they hit, and of the rose, and of the word *rose*,
and of the streetmarket bowl of roses on his writing-table this
otherwise grimed-over day in the late spring on Mickle Street, the book
he's writing, the room around a book or even a single poem
that's through now though the song itself, the cellsong
and the sunspotsong, is never through, and
we will sing the praises of you
and you will sing the praises of us, too.

Second Level

Some of the anticounterfeiting devices themselves have been
counterfeited.
                    —Bruce W. Most

José Oliveira, a human, was the voice of José Carioca
the parrot. The parrot samba'd limegreen-assed
down the carnival streets of Rio, singing, explaining.
This was 1942. The Disney studio was making South America
real to Springfield, Cleveland, Dubuque (the U.S.
needing new, non-European, markets). And so Oliveira,
for *his* brief festive-plumaged moment, joined
the Golden Voices: Pinto Colvig (Goofy), Clarence
("Ducky") Nash. It might be true—as the 13th-century
bestiary says—the beak of a parrot is hard, enough
"so if you throw down the bird from a height,
to a rock, it lands on the beak in safety." But in any
case, Oliveira must have thought, the beak of a parrot
isn't easy—and he'd try again to prise himself
persuasively into that saffron clamp of a mouth
on the thinglet they showed him off their storyboard drawings:
perky, eye-cocked, panama-hatted. And after a day
of being a voice between wings (that were arms and ended
in hands that held a furled umbrella), in the back nook
of a café, sated, brandied, cigared, he must have thought

———

how intricately crazy it was, to be a man who simulates
a bird who simulates a man... And this, then, is his place
in the ubiquity of fakery's taking on second-level expression.
Also, the one-time camouflaging confetti of woodsy colors,
lichen-like and mossish, of the peppered-moth: is over generations
sullen brown, with which it matches its background's being
denuded and grimed by industrial air. And also,
William Henry Ireland's evidently brilliantly-emulatory
forgeries of Shakespeare (Boswell kneeled and kissed them; Sheridan
purchased *Vortigern*, produced it at Drury Lane): when
they were proved dupe texts, they entered a respectable collectors' fame
of their own, and Ireland flooded the market with forgeried

70

forgeries—"sham shams," Andrew Lang said. And also,
the mild, deceiving color of the antarctic petrel, an ice-gray blue
that blends it like an ingredient into the large bland batter
of ocean spume and leaden coastal sky: has been appropriated,
after study, for U.S. Navy camouflage color "Omega Gray." And
also, that opulent decoy-body of sepia ink a cuttlefish forges its
own shape with: is just the thing for hoaxing the faded
look of centuries into this morning's drawings... As if the rule

———

reads, *A mask by its very origin-energy must*
become mask-two. The rule applies. And also, we
apply it. Do you remember that day at the flea market? I
can see, still, where those sloppy rows of vendors' tables thinned,
and gravel claimed its frugal space, for small replenishing:
cokes, a pungent "Porta-John," the recounting of change.
I don't remember why I brought that hurt look
over my face—though in those days I imagined it carried a
brisk veneer of "irony," whatever that was; I worked the
greater part of my emotive signals into its range. And maybe that's
why your own eyes showed such anger so immediately—the edge
of new impatience with my old displays. I had no choice,
then, but indifference, and I slipped it into place
with the ease of a deejay playing hurt's flip side.
So then it was your turn for hurt. Then mine, for anger...
Chance (some lucky buy; a stranger's stare) might stop
that escalation—did. But while it exists it's horrific
progression, our faces growing more false and insistent by
rapidchange stages and everywhere vendors hawked their pirated
secondhand piles of shiny vinyl leathergoods. Oh the rule

———

applies, the rule applies... In a film, here's Hitler's Poland
and two near-witless, broken, elderly Jews seek refuge
in a theater. It's Nazi High Command performance night,
the audience: row on row of swastika'd Jew-killers,
hundreds. Ah, but there's a clown scene. Pompommed and ruffed
with the cast, they dance plain-view down center aisle,
safe escape out the lobby just prances away. Though half-way

71

down, about row J, the grandma panics and lets out a soulful,
disclosing, Yiddish scream... And that's only the first level.
Though it's crazy enough—as, say, the "real world" of "real
parrots" is crazy enough without cartoon extrapolation. In
New Zealand there's a flightless parrot, the kakapo, that burrows
like a rabbit. The German explorer Humboldt says
in South America he met "a parrot that had the only knowledge
of a dead language, the entire tribe of Indians who
spoke it having become extinct." The parrot of the
Maharajah of Nawanagar had a golden built-in Rolls Royce perch
"and an international passport." Truly. No wonder
Oliveira's lifting another drink—as if to bid a fond farewell
to being a persona, in this poem—with a benign

———

bemusement softening his face: the lovely/terrifying/miraculous
multilayering of world on world! It's 1942. In the film,
the clown in front of them savvily turns, presents the Nazis
a histrionic conspiratorial wink, points at the couple
(explaining *Jews!*—GRIN—*Jews!*) and with one of those circus-troupe
flag-shooting guns, he marches them out of the theater, to safety,
the audience lost in guffaws. —And so the truth on top
of the guilefulness on top of the truth sufficed. I have a
brilliantly colored Sunday-comics page from 1944: José
Carioca the parrot, disguised in what looks like a mop
(for a blonde wig) and a grass skirt, is aiding the effort against
the Axis, involved in some kind of dangerous Amazon tropics
skullduggery ("I've got to theenk op som'theeng, queeck!").
It's one of who-knows-how-many serial episodes, so
makes the most limited sense. But when I saw it scream
its jungle-parrot colors from the flea market clutter
—a real buy in junksville—well, my heart was won.
Whatever love it allowed, we drove home smiling
—remember? The parrot badguy is playing into Carioca's
limegreen hands. On this level there will be a happy ending.

Matchbox

The sun is filtered down to amber webwork
in a plastic mug of plastic amber beer
a half-inch high, in the House
of Miniatures. Nearby: an inch-long taco
with a bite taken out and a brown ooze of generic
taco-plasm, rubbery, puddled around it
—someone's thought of everything. The masters
on the wall: Van Gogh's The Starry Night the size
of a stamp, as if his astral visionary pattern is here
transistorized. The Mona Lisa. Picasso's
Old Man with Guitar. There is no end to small:
because there's a garden the size of my hand,
there's also one emigré flower of it set in a pot
the size of my littlest nail. And I understand
by now so well that a bee the size for the sexual
landing-strips and furzy undersweets of that flower
of course exists, I can imagine the pollen
abundantly clustered about its hips, each grain
a golden oval that could open, a piñata, and
genetic-code spirals come showering down.

———————

That summer I worked the loading docks I saw
how Fleischer's glories and despondencies were fitted
to the daily count of herring barrels, and one bedraggled
diner coffee-pourer named Dolores whose lowslung rump
kept up his wolf-howl and moth-flutter all night
—these encouraged in him exquisite bluesy eruptions
of song as articulate as any expression I've heard before
or since from those whose wants and losses are measured
in the buying and selling of nation-states.
He'd sing and the sea would stop a moment. And seeing
these barrels of thimble girth in the matchbox truck
this morning, I could hear a tinny version of his basso,
a filament quavering in the air above this landscape—it
sufficed, being poignant to its universe's
scale. In these homes not much looks used (the taco
notwithstanding)—sheets on these beds of notepad dimension

never come stained. But on the workbench a microscope no
larger than a raisin magnifies *something*: the leg of a flea
like a hairdresser's comb; the dance, and all it means,
of sperm and egg, to the music the moon even moves to.

———————

It was snug where he sat, and the waxy back curve
snaked with hot gray conduits, hugging him
—Thumbkin, in the Grimm tale, seated tailorwise
in a horse's ear. *Gee up,* he says
(in one translation) "and they were amazed at a dobbin
plowing without the farmer anywhere!" How old
is that amazement? How old are the stories in Grimm?
They've always been with us, the little ones. *Pygmy*
is ancient Greek—"the distance from the elbow
to the knuckles of a normal-sized man." But they date
farther, the little ones. The heartwood
of a bristlecone pine can be 5,000 years and it isn't
enough. Farther. They've always been with us,
in us, fallopian-us: that small, and still
transmitting the lifebeat. That summer, I had a
waitress too, a pal of Fleischer's girl's. And she had a
husband. The noonbreak look of the bed in the House
of Miniatures brings it all back: a threshold,
my standing there torn two ways,
then a voice in my ear and I enter.

———————

Unwilled, the smallness appalls: consider Gulliver
growing nauseous as the pitted nipple-surface at the peak
of a whale-stink Brobdingnagian bosom stiffens gnarled
to his waist. Though willed, it pleasures us past any
moderation: think of a time and place where women willingly
bound their feet, despite the blood and sloughing;
competed for daintiness; referred to them
as "Chestnut Blossoms"; and men, in sexual ardor, took them
wholly into their mouths. If it sounds aberrant
it wasn't, in its time and place—the full grace
of a culture was applied to this "Exquisite Diminution."

At best, we have to feel ambivalent; so saying *small*
calls forth its only modification, *relatively*.
The mites that thrive in our eyelashes have,
in photomega-enlargement, all the clumsy thrust of slogging
water buffalo, and are huger than the sex of light
and brain by which we see them. Men joke about
"big" but what does it mean? She made me feel "big."
Then I heard that her husband drove right off the pier
on purpose. I'd never felt so small.

———————

A bonsai is plenty. When wind moves nearly
a human sigh through one, I think a lung
and its branches is just that size. And under such
a bough, a Thumbkin rests at last, breathes out, and
tries to place his late adventures in proportion—sacrifice,
thievery, and more. The key is always proportion. What
if I'd told you their names, their ages?
But then they'd be sized to some other poem. If the key
is proportion, any door will do. This one in the house
in the House of Miniatures leads out to a garden
with one tree I can imagine some homunculus-me
beneath, in meditation. I might be someone's
homunculus-me myself. Well if he's watching let me
simply walk the ridge to a bristlecone pine. If time
can be a size, this tree's immense. If size
can ever be a wisdom, it's here, in this heart
that was green when the first baked pottery figurines
—the first rough dolls and their objects—were done. Now
let me hug that trunk, let me pattern my arms with its
pattern, from knuckles up to crook-pulse—my *pygmy*.

"A Deep and Craving Hunger...for the Past"

—Eric Larsen, *Writing and Nostalgia*

And so she looked back. Remembering
the blue smoke ropes uncoiling from the camel-patty fires;
her mealy wheeling of chickpea-and-oil through its cedar bowl;
the wallcloths, with that odor of goat in them deep as a dye;
and how, in even those days before the angels came to their door
in the sandals of men, there was an especially mysterious immanence,
rich and just this side of tactile, in the quality of the shadows of
that place and time. She may have right now remembered it with
the poignancy finality gives fondness—a memory
maybe already sweetened away from stark historical fact
by a kind of phychological pastry-glaze... and
so we might say she's turned to a pillar

of sugar as accurately as we might say salt. Nostalgia.
How it works; and how it works on us. In books, in film,
the list of people counseled to not look back or forever
be weakened is legion. Some do anyway: the legion
of the lost. For instance, Ashley. It's a good name, all that's sacred
to him torched at Yankee hands. The new world's brick;
the very mercantile souls of its inhabitants will never burn, or
even be inflamed by anything much. And when his
poor ewe-like transparent eyes reveal the start of the longing again
for the crinoline world of the garden parties and courtly ado,
well, Scarlett's here with her linear strength to stay him
in the present, its vitality, crudeness, ledgerbooks. I saw it

at the Royal, where the inside ceiling gleamed with stars
like a jeweler's black-satin-backed tray, and ushers paraded
gold-braided uniforms of maharajah splendor. I was
10 and it was 1958. The grilles and headlights of the cars
made human faces. The pharmacist knew every one of his
customers by name and need, and there was a penny
candy counter with cherry licorice whips and those small wax
replicas of sodapop bottles filled with cloying swigs. When I
look back it's all a sepia blur (that early Kodak color I've learned
over time to think of the past as) then I focus and individual
objects redden or blue, and eventually are true to the primary
colors chart on the wall of 5th grade Home Room. For nostalgia

76

is selective. Who remembers Bender "Alleyway,"
the nigger valet from the Royal john, who when they
closed the theater—I was college age by then—fucked hens
for a dollar at fraternity parties? I'll tell you:
nobody. There was never a hall rug ruined by blood
and filthy anal feathers, then rolled up into a long log carried
straight out of the neural memory-record. The family name
was Talleyweight, and goes back to a famous plantation
countinghouse in Ashley's day, as history
can prove, because it's history's place to save the lives
of the dead. But it's nostalgia's place to save the living
from their own lives, and it does, and it glows, and I'm going

to write about Djanek Zfaney. It's 8 pm. He bars
his pharmacy doors against the whole dull see you later
alligator of 1958. Lush summer dusk. Feet propped
on the counter, he hums. And then he sings, to the pills and the gauzes,
some thread of the words. It isn't English, this. *Sausage*, he sings,
in somewhere else's word for sausage. *Fountain*. *Bird*. A time
takes place about that sausage, fountain, bird—its stone paths
at the harbor, an accordion player, a woman's face in light
a lost world sifts through like a bathroom talcum... *Bird*, the word
he savors, *bird*. The mothertongue on his tongue. *Bird* a flan or
bird a marzipan, a liveable pain, these little pockets
of sugar, the caries. His only sweetness. *Bird*. His only

weakness and strength.

Neologisms

Outage is recent. "Northwest sector Seventeen reports
a power outage." So is *slippage*. "Unit seven downscaled
the cable slippage to four-oh-three." *Homunculus* is less
new, *bioengineering* more. Though mean the same categorical
thing: below the dispassionate light of the stars
one night, a man will suddenly see how his body is
landscape, lush and enterable, and he'll burn to be a pilgrim
down its arterial torrents and millruns, to whatever
watery shrine his time considers an ultimate answer; and there
will be new language code-keyed to the journey's seeming

newness. "Green-shit! Dirty-rotten-toilet-devil!"
—Chimps, and the invention of invective. At the Center
for teaching primates American Sign Language, Washoe
and friends (on their own) have discovered words are stackable
units, and like the vertical registers of ancient Egyptian art, add
up, dimensionally, to a world and its workings: here,
a swan on a pond, the term is "waterbird," invented from its two
component nouns by someone who's picking her tummy
for fleas just now, then chucking a bananaskin down
the lines of this poem. And someone's flicking a bug in his mouth

—it's Darwin. "One day, on tearing off some old bark, I
saw two rare beetles, and seized one in each hand; then I saw a
third and new kind, which I could not bear to lose, so that
I popped the one which I held in my right hand into my mouth."
And when it's carefully slipped back out through pursed lips,
it will shine not only with harsh South American sun,
its own black mica-like wings, and the naturalist's salivas, but
with the radiance of anything new, its first time out
(for which I invent the word *newminous*); and its nomenclature,
Latinate and popular, will similarly shine the first time

flying unsteadily out of the mouth responsible. And
so "sky scraper!" "DNA!" "sonic boom!" Out of the first,
an old man with a cane is walking laboriously, and normally
this fresh banana peel dropped from somewhere wouldn't
matter. But there's been a power outage: it's dark. Soon,
sadly, slippage will occur. And he's the neighborhood's
last repository of certain verbal loveliness: *halcyon,*
nostrum, antimacassar. In his own new days, this peel
might mean Keaton, Chaplin, swooping through a medium itself
so new, there weren't words. But now it's later and everyone

new in his building is busy so won't hear his minimal
animal-moan of pain. Their own expression, though, is similar
vocabulary: under a vibrator's high hum is a long-drawn low
of pleasure; in a pink room is the abstract crooning-to-sleep
of the baby, who still, in his dribble and diaperslops, is miles
away from his first, half-formed, initiatory speech. And
here's an old man, hurt. No "mustard-plaister" will help.
No "microsurgery," unless somebody hurries. Now from
the cave at the deep of his throat, from mammal-grease
and sea salts, an old word, one of the oldest, and darkest,

slips out.

Reading In

*...a foisting of our sentiments onto an inert
and indifferent scenery.*
—Helen Vendler

1.
And then I said the bus's wheels in fresh
Chicago snow left long
albino alligators. I said it was
happy snow. I know, I was reading
into things again. You were with me,
you kissed me under a lamp post growing
a skullcap of snow as white as the Pope's, so
I wasn't surprised that it blessed us.
It winked. It had a light and it winked.
The snow against the sky was white and then
against the cone of wattage was black. That's
true, that's photographically exact. And
the post, I know, was a post: pure,
and with a globe of glass on top that was pure and
beyond interpretation. I know that.
Snow is water knitted a little tighter,
that's all, and I know that too. It's water
doilies, that's all. It's a statement of physics.
But look: it gave itself up
to the night, to something
larger, with an easy resignation anybody
would have to call happy. It shone,
it was happy snow, some landed on your tongue
and that was happy, happy snow.

2.
Then why do we cringe at the world of willows
bent in bereavement, mercury rising slim and
passionately up thermometers, the abnegation
of bone-white Japanese tea cups? There were
cultures where the wind in the bough was your future.
The leaves on the stream were your future.
The gut of a sheep.
The cracks burnt into a tortoise shell.

80

The gut of a bull. The gut of a peacock.
Even now, a man is thinking his own mood
into the wind, then thinking the wind is a forecast.
How many leaves in a tree, how many
small green hands, are scrubbing up like surgeons
in wind? And he'll call it a feeling, a hunch,
"in my gut." Now the shadows of Japanese tea cups
are a portrait of ripening plums, precisely. Now
they're the loose gray fannings in silt
a fishtail clears for the spawning.
Now they're dragged back into their cups,
black slips drawn up below white uniforms.
The nothing-gut of a slug.
The gut of a whale hung up like a tabernacle.

3.
Up the road from the whaleworks, maybe an hour
by horse then ferry, is the woolen-mill and
up the shale walkway is its miller. For him,
the blades are an enormous, steady
timepiece; wool is his weather, the time is always
simply life o'clock. He loves his hands
in the sorting-bin. They lose direction in wool as a hundred
years later, astronauts will float
in space—no "up" or "down." He loves his wife
lost just that way, a woman in the odor
and money and buffer-against-December
of wool, of angeltufts of wool to grade in their baskets.
These are the days of their lives:
some wool, more wool, bad wool, good.

*

In a different place, and time, a different man
will put an end to that. Out of his own and only
life, with its consistent rat-jawed gnawings of failure,
its lover with the blue tattoo and the little tube of gel,
its precision, its decade in the lab, its deliberate turnings,
he'll invent a blend of synthetic fibers,
newer, better. And so these two are nexus-points
defining a narrative line, though they

81

don't know it, though neither sees right now
the worm-holes through the newel of the abandoned mill,
its frost-cracked shelf of baskets. But
these two are points—of my plot and yours. It's
what we do to the stars—read in

*

the catscradle interconnection of story
up there, as an earthworm reads,
by total braille,
its wants and horrors into its sky
our planet. We read in: monstrousness
and grace. A throne. A weapon. A wedding. Yes and
at last we read our needings so
emphatically and crosshatched
into the sky, we call it heaven, and
our reading ends in
translating ourselves. / Listen:

*

weeping. Simply, he's weeping
the morning away in his hands. Simply,
she's died—the miller's wife. And now
the black-toothed tortoise chignon-comb on the bureau
is an eloquent mouth with an eloquent history
issuing, it could drive a man to tears.
And now he walks with a special acuity
to his vision: all of February
ice and shadow is edged as if it's stropped
past fineness. It snows. It
snows. He witnesses the absolute spider
spinning at the center of those absolute webs.
And he sees where she's gone to: the wings,
the harp, the headware like an o of honey,
her face in a cloud.

*

Heaven, in some Turkish illustration, is a garden
flowered bottom to top like a silk gown: raw pink
blooms the unvarying size of lettuces, divvying up blue background.

82

The perspective is shaky: an angel
opening orange wings as rigid as the side-leaves of a table
snapped open when guests arrive, is either walking
lightly through the middle distance or flying
by taking standard child-sized steps through the air.
A camel kneels. Three other camels talk
by touching noses while their riders exchange bouquets.
And somebody's riding a deer
with the face of a beautiful woman
through a cloud of fire, or into a pool of chased gold.
It's more recognizable over Medieval Europe:
here's St. Peter holding his familiar key as heavy
and ornate as a Flash Gordon ray-gun, here's
the heavenly choir around His throne in rows
of schoolroom order, and here's the bordering
glow of gauzy ochers shot with amber licks
that means The Glory. This

*

is the other world, as it once must have been
above the world of plowing, riding, swimming
in a real place, in a real time: "August," say,
from *Les Trés Heures du Duc de Berry,*
15th century, France. The land is complicated
yellows leading to deep green tufts that mean
the beginnings of trees, then hills. It isn't easy
walking once the slopes go steep, and especially
by November, when the leaves are a lovely layer
covering dips and twists. By now our breath
is grayish shapes in the air, like a glassblower's.
Night comes on. You shiver—I've read us
into this world—and so we walk half-hugging.
It snows. It muffles everything—cows,
Toyotas, who knows? You lean on a lamp post.
The stars are a scintillant pollen,
burning but austere! Or that's the zodiac
of fresh Chicago snow
in the black expanse of your hair.

83

The Real War

1.
"You overboiled chucklump of soupmeat"—good
Shakespearian bile in a China hotel. "Go diddle
a flophouse lobby socket"—better by far
than our own last night's halfhearted cliché purveying
of "oh you bitch" and "bastard." What a couple! He's
heaving out with a kodiak bear's magenta-eyed ferocity and
she's meeting it with a diva's imperturbable
iron-breasted Viking brio, air gone
"dwindledick!" and "fumblecunt!", and all this
on a sunlit terrace backdropped by a tapestry
of some dozen redundant contemplative views of Mt. Fuji
rising serenely out of clouds, while a hotel crew,
schooled and uniformed for semblance of servility,
flutterhovers about like hummingbirds having
discovered mad rats in the honeywater. Her
top lip's bruised. His right cheek's scratched
wide open. We can only sit here stuck
with the rest of the breakfast crowd, in muzzy
stupefaction at this crazy world, where the shadowed
backalley apothecaries are opening up for a day
of powdered rhino horn and hundred-year-old doveseggs,
and the mighty technological expertise of Taiwan
is stamping out its store of America's rubber noses,
joy buzzers, squirting roses, wee-wee statuettes.

2.
And the days repeat. And the nights repeat.
And the bud of moon is eventually a lemon-white willowware
dinnerplate reflected in the Canton River, bright enough
to read by. We're on the balcony. "Listen to what this says."
The "Son of Heaven," the Chinese Emperor, pleasured the Empress,
3 "consorts," 9 "spouses," then 27 "concubines" and their
81 "assistants"—in an intricate, official
"rotation of duty." I rhapsodize cinnabar bevies of redheads,
wheatfield blondes, tight anthracite ebonycoifs,
a harem: "now *that's* variety." "He didn't do it"
you look up "for variety. He did it for the sameness."
You let me think about it. We argue a bit. I go

84

walk the rim of the pool. You're right. I halve them like
an antfarm, and in each of those women, slipping aroused
beneath the imperial silks, is only the same
hormonal display up the ducts and their tubules. Never
thinned by reverie, never complicated by phase.
Now back in our room, I wonder if change and stasis isn't
the real war, that keeps the universe balanced and fueled.
Later, we make our own love—not the legendary love
of kings and queens perhaps, but full moon limns
our ampersanded skins just fine. It's hard to think of something
this lush as stunted, though it would be of course if kept
full every evening. Cycleless—opulent, yes, but deprived.

3.
And this is sleekest bedsheet silk, that's a mulberry leaf redone
in the gut of a silkworm. And this is the leaf, and this is the
dynasty of leaves redone from dynasties of people
tucked in burial silks... These easy links of changing
keep me sleepless. I go to the pooledge again. Its far side
sparks and writhes—some man and woman don't see me or
see and can't care; I hear their hackneyed sweetsing,
"baby, ooh" and "do me, do" and one black silhouette leans deeply
in another like a picker's ladder into a ripe-ready bough.
In this genericness of ardor, they could be
us, or anyone, "yes yes oh"... And this is the sheen the sky makes
of sweat and chlorine on their flesh. And this is the sky,
the wheel, the clock of burning white giants and red dwarves.
This is light through the milky width of the galaxy, nothing
a mind can encompass. And these are the pages of Earth, pressing
mountains as we press flowers. No wonder we need imagining
Time that's manageable, a unit we can hold: a single
pitchpipe breath, a fetus's heartbeat, sonnets, dice,
the waist of an odalisque night after night. I think
we're all conscriptees in the real war, of simply remaining
ourselves through the passage we call our days.
For instance, these two poolside lovers... done, and dried,
they hand-in-hand approach me—that same
couple, from breakfast. Empires fall. The sun sets. Empires rise.

Cathay

Such is my nature: I enjoy sitting up through the night, often with a book under the candle. Tonight I put the book down and sat calmly, untroubled, surrounded by silence. A long rain had just purified the sky, a pale moon was shining. And after a while, I could hear sounds.

The ever onward rustling of the wind in the bamboo. The snarling of dogs, as if barring out evil. The sound of drums and then a bell, pure and clean through rain-cleared air. With it came thoughts of dawn, of rising and doing, though it was still night.

Our reaching an equilibrium where these sounds can be heard, where the outside world and the inner calm are at one, brings a cleansing of mind and of spirit.

This happens seldom. But one should remember: it is not that at other times these sounds do not exist. It is that sitting up through the night allows a special reception.

—reworked from Shen Chou
above his painting *The Night Vigil*
* dated 1492 *

1.

That same year, Columbus

"set sail" "across the boundless main" "for the Orient"
—the way we heard it in grammar school. And it must have been

approximately true, those 3 construction paper
ships in primary colors, and their primary captain

standing at the prow with a hand raised to shield his eyes,
giving them the slightly shadowed space—just out
of this world's strictest maritime field of light—in which a more

visionary seeing occurs. An inch
of mysterious twilight. Even without that

obvious silhouette, that clear accommodating of every
new-met degree of longitude and latitude
to an interior map, we know he saw

by inspiration as truly as he saw by navigational rule,
the compass, the ledger, the sovereignly decree. *By many miracles*
He hath shown me, I believe I might be employed to discover
Paradise itself, or more. Yet for all that

he was a worldly, practical man; and even the zealous religious fires
inside him were used to power the small machine of imperial acquisi-
tiveness he became and tended—as all such machinery must be—with
the oils of practiced unctuousness. By marriage he connected himself
to the Portuguese royal family. It was Spain, of course, that finally
backed his mission. *Profit, finance, treasure*—these are the words that
tediously repeat in his appeals to the court, which needed lucre for
its war against the Moors. It's likely Columbus joined the army while
waiting an answer, and helped dispatch his share of infidels. It's
certain he worked the religious angle: let him sail, and all the fabled
wealth of Cathay could enable a Spanish crusade to win the Holy
Sepulcher at Jerusalem back for Christendom. (And infidels would
be barred, from the start, from the new, Castilian Indies—and Jews,
and "heretics" and "foreigners" of all kinds. This is made clear in his
suggestions on colonization.) He was shrewd at sea. He kept 2 sets
of records—one his own, and one of sugared statistics to mollify his
men. He was hard. His answer to storms was bread-and-water pen-
ances. And—it has to be said—he wanted the glory. Juan Rodriguez
Bermejo, "marinero de la *Pinta*," was the one who shouted at 2 in
the morning "Tierra! Tierra!" Columbus claimed, and got, the reward
of 10,000 maravedis. (The books don't indicate Bermejo's response.)
And all through the islands, Columbus's eye was alive in the most
pragmatic way for exhibitions of his success. The natives were "very
cowardly, fit to be ordered about and made to work, to sow and do
aught else that may be needed." (On a later voyage he'd capture 500
to send to Spain as slaves—of which 200 died en route and were
pitched like refuse into the ocean.) The report in which he'd sum-
marize his labor is a savvy appeal to avarice and sensationalism. The
people are "handsome and well-formed" and "the women cover only
one place with the leaf of a plant. Of anything they have, if you ask

them for it, they never say no." There are "great mines of gold."
There will be "great refreshment and profit. Merely the men of one
of my ships could destroy that whole country." (This would, in a
way, become true—50 years later, there weren't more than 500 of
Haiti's original 300,000 inhabitants alive there.) And this report he'd
send to the monarchs on March 14, 1493, via—appropriately—their
Keeper of the Privy Purse. But

now it's 1492, and possible

to like him. Because it's Friday, the 3rd of August,
in the first, small, orange hours
of a day, and he's checking the thick pitch coat at the waterline.
With his gold braid cap. With his eyes that saw
a rock in the shape of a horseman
pointing west (he must have been 20 then) and this,
he knew, was a sign. With the smell of dew on the decks
in his nostrils; dew, and a barrel of salt-pork strips,
and a sack of the last of the chiseled barnacles.
With his volume of Marco Polo. Because I really
don't want to defame him. With his compass needle
turning in his gut. Because he's overseeing
the fastening of the ballast stones. Because his faith
was a stone, that he never let drop. Because he was right.
Because he died in terrible anguish because he was right.
With the sails, for just this moment, as roseate as petals,
from the sun. Because it's Friday, the 3rd of August,

1492, and the first, far, chalkpowder stars
are in the sky, in China. Shen Chou

sets his book down, feels. Something
is happening. Shapes are losing
definition, giving their hardest edges up
to night. Where there was rock before, and water...
now there's the mingle-space of rock's and water's being held
in a greater, ambiguous substance. If he closes his eyes
and concentrates—no, if he closes his eyes and
doesn't concentrate, avidly doesn't concentrate over time
and over distance... he can feel himself give up himself
that same way, and whatever remains

above the book that's irreducibly left in the light, might think
some sweetly pitying thing about the creatures,
rocks and water and men, that live by day, that even by night
live mainly by day, with its partitions and its strictures.
Blessed be the break of day

(the deck-boy's singing now)
And the Holy Cross, by which we pray.
God bless this voyage. Anchors aweigh!
With his letter of introduction to the Grand Khan of the Indies.
With his charts. With the sharp-sided sun in his eyes.
It was night, in Cathay. With his astrolabe.
With the royal comptroller along, to parse the gold.
With the teasing prospectus of gold.
He called it *otro mundo*. It was night there,

it was the other world.

2.

This fleet of good hope sailed parallel to another fleet of misery and woe. On the very same tide there dropped down the Saltés the last vessel carrying the Jews whom Ferdinand and Isabella had expelled from Spain. August 2 was their deadline; any who remained thereafter were to be executed unless they embraced Christianity.
                                                            —Samuel Eliot Morison

Dear God and God of my fathers, faith,
    I know, should be a constant
undiminished by flurry amongst the points along this daily plane
    of mortal exertions. These are terms
I pluck, in haste too huge for epistolary finesse,
    from the algebraicus, of which I know a little.
Do You know what it is, to have the books of your study bundled
    like slops for the hound? I worked a year once,
hauling vats of ashes for the tallowers, to purchase an astrologicker
    with proper tables and indices. And so You will understand
that I wept. Do You know even
    what it is, to be a horse? You will pardon these questions.
You know, I know, what everything is. Or You know,
    I *believe*, what everything is, which is a difference
worthy of an evening's meditation—but for necessary hurry
    and these sores along my arm the soldiers supplied as a ready
mnemonic device, in case I forget the departure, and so it
    hurts to grip the pen. I kept it out, however, and these few
rags of paper, and the inkhorn—everything else, as You know,
    and foresaw, and allowed, is a bundle now. My daughter
is a bundle, and we slung her at the horse's ribs
    like any sack of clothes or pantry silver. She is only two,
and cried. Because I write to You,
    my weeping is my own; but she is new to speech, and previous, still,
to the most of speech, and so her tears may be her
    praying, to which I beseech You, listen: for Yours is its
intended ear. A sailor is showing her knots, now.
    Now the horse, that all day carried a house
become dishevelment, is leaning its long, sienna head
    against a stucco wall and I know what it is
to rest a head like one more in a pile of heavy
    bags of useless objects.

*

And I am from such fathers, O God
    of my fathers...! I must tell You now I thought
when a child, helping sickle then pile the sheaves, that You were
    the sun. (They told me You were everywhere, and
watching, and in every living thing, and drew us to You but
    could grow wroth.) So You will remember shining
on Todros Ben Judah Abulafia, singer to the court
    of Sancho Fourth, whose verses I have yet in my oilcloth packet
and save against a time of need for his brief, sleek, birdsong sweetness,
    and on Don Samuel ha-Levi Abulafia, chief treasurer under
Pedro First... Forgive me. It is not these bauble
    accomplishments themselves. They mean a something
endures, in fixity, beyond the whimsy fortune
    of a single life; and our holding to this
idea of continuing may be our chiefmost
    semblance to Your image. I have thought about this
long. (They told me You were the lamp in the synagogue
    in every seed, that You were in the honeycomb, the warren
of hairs in the nostril, the lentil, the marrowbone, the weed,
    the buttery bead left at the teat-tip after milking...) At
noon, my caped back to the crew as if I squatted
    green from the first wind-roughened waters, I unbundled
so much of the family wares—an incense pan, a coals-plate,
    seven chalices—not for the gold though they
were gold, but for the line of Abulafias
    they come down, and this is a comfort. The sun
was a flame in the side of each of the chalices.
    This made a candelabrum. There is no wind so rough on this or any water
it can snuff such flames.

*

One night is gone—my
    daughter is already
foreign to me. She says no, and no, but I see that
    yes, her hair we combed in two harsh, beautiful raven's wings
is sienna. Perhaps from a day of unnatural
    bondage to the horse. The world will
color us in—*we* are *its* map. These perfect burgundy
    bruises up my arm will be a weak lime
by the Netherlands. When yesterday
    three royal-bannered caravels passed our side, their sailors

danced on a barrel, and sang, and made my little Racheleh laugh. Now
    she sings *Holy Cross, by which we pray*—the words they taught her.
This is a problem I set to You, for it is far beyond
    my meager algebraicus. If we leave the same shore, on the same
stinking ship, and in one another's arms, how is it, God
    of my fathers, my daughter is traveling
into a new world so quickly?

*

You will recognize this. I am but the latest
    Abulafia to turn its pages. This, here?—when a boy,
it was my favorite. Is it accurate? My people
    look fresh, the straw sacks on their shoulders must hold goods
the weight of air. And You have parted the towering waters
    of the Red Sea with a meticulous ease, as, elsewhere,
Ruth, and Naomi, and elsewhere Bathsheba, part their hair.

*

...and waiting more. We took this as a time to scrape
    these weeks of puke, and the scales of it filled two buckets.
Later they brought the news. And so with Netherlandish
    welcome turned away from us, we will attempt an overland
journey eastward to the Orient. I am wrong and my bruises
    deepen. I am tired, and my daughter is tired. Do You know
even, what it is, to move from your center? You are
    entirely center, unto Your edge, which is also Your center.
(They told me this.) And so You are the sun
    at last, that is itself as long as light is long,
and as complete. But we who have moved, and must yet move
    come morning, ask You to look at Your children
the stars. By their motionless bodies, we travel. And
    how much burning they need to suffer, to scream in quiet, to throw
by fiery handfulls, what great energy and dying,
    just to remain in place!

3.

I didn't know what tribe, what red percent
of it, but by the way the flat rise
of her cheekbones turned the urban light to plainslight,
vast with the shimmer of distance and beast-heat, I
wasn't surprised when she told me she was an Indian,
winked, and whispered "You know—ancient knowledge." It
seemed auspicious enough; a month of facing tables
in the library, and tonight—result of 15 minutes' nervy
flirting powwow—we had a dinner date. I daydreamed naked
tom-tom dances about a bedroom bonfire, with the black
lash of her squaw-braid reaching her ass. I was
20; that's some of what it is to be 20. And this is a story

of what I studied, that year in a library nook: Columbus's
early reports on the natives. This is an exam in that course:
1) "They say on one island the people gather gold on the beach
by candlelight and hammer it into bars." 2) "And there is a
ring in these Indies, to place it under the tongue will render
anyone invisible." 3) "One tribe eats human flesh: we found
great cuts but partly-devoured, and young boys *a castrati* being
plumped in cages." 4) "Also there were bulls, with horns
of iron, and these ferocious beasts were sometimes green, now
black, now red, now yellow." 5) "Of their fruits, the best is
armored like a knight; and there is a great leaf that they burn and
drink the smoke thereof." (I interrupt this exam

to bring you a test of this poem's Civil Defense Emergency
Broadcast Signal: xxxxxxxxxx. Thank you. In the event
of a real emergency, you'd be dead. To continue:) 6) "A magic
herb, its juices allay every spasm and harmful hurt."
7) "The men saw mermaids, though not so beautiful as those
disporting alluringly in paintings." 8) "And a tribe,
their ears are long to their knees." 9) "In such ways
they hunt turtle: by a trained fish, on a leash, and it
attaches by a sucker to its prey which the Indians then do
just haul in." 10) "Of the men there, some are horned
and have no speech, but grunt, like pigs; although their
parrots discourse like scholars." Now tell me which

5 here are fact, as logged by Columbus, and which are
willful fiction (Mandeville, 1356; also the Orlando series,
1483–1532). You see? And how real was I, there
at her door? In a growing global nuclear insanity I was,
I'm sure to either side, a microdot in a dot on a strategy-grid
as seen from the height of a cloud-layer. Then her painter
neighbor passed: I was a flask in which a window decanted
a pour of that passionate saffron-orange sun can be. To
the sun? to the timeless intercellular passage of neutrinos?:
I was universe-stuff of a certain amalgam and density.
To me, I was eager, sensitive, hesitant, foolish, loony to enter
her sexual wigwam. Then she answered the door in her

sari and bing cherry caste-mark. You see? The
answer is: 1) 3) 5) 7) 9)...as "fact." It is in *my* world,
anyway. To the "Indios," Columbus and his men arrived
"from the sky," on creatures with massive, white wings (in a
way, they came from someplace unimaginably farther
than the sky, which is, in any land, intangible and awesome
but indigenous). While the first illustrated European edition
of his report, in 1493, depicted Columbus landing
from a 40-oar Mediterranean galley. Any -time,
-place, -person or -event must be the nexus of unlimited
coeval, incompatible perceptions, and a wife in bed I might
ignore one night busy collating notes for a "Columbian sonnet,"

I might need near me intimately and fiercely the
next, the same wife and the same me but the sky
can make a difference. There were B-52's in their needley
lift and stitch above Bergstrom Air Force Base—we, none
of us, is ever sure we'll see tomorrow, and this mundane
appraisal of the overriding horror, when it's clear, makes anything
less than love inadequate. And something—light refracted
in the shadows of her sleep—brought back an extravagant
lotus pinned in the hair of a woman 15 years ago, then minutes
later undone and set on her sari on the floor. We were
there, though transported worlds away from there, I think in what
here always is: somewhere else's unimportance, somewhere

else's exotica.

4.

Those who came before—how close do we feel to them, do we *really* feel to them? My students often can't empathize much with the 60's spirits that informed the swings of the Vietnam war; too many changes of fashion and cultural sensibility intervene, too many alternations of the guru and the corporate executive as identity-models. Thomas Mann, in *Joseph and His Brothers*, suggests that at one time (he's back in Old Testament days) a changelessness existed that we can think of as less a stasis and more a field of continuity with the past: "...on the whole time then had been more conservatively minded than time now... Memory, resting on oral tradition from generation to generation, was more direct and confiding, it flowed freer, time was a more unified and thus a briefer vista." Perhaps the Neolithic Revolution first disrupted this unity. But even by the relatively recent past—by 1492, say—we can look at paintings of Biblical scenes and see that time has been tucked up close, like a blanket we can fold, and so shorten: patriarchs, angels, martyrs are defined by the dress and attitudes of their painters. Maybe the species-memory, even now, isn't at home with the idea of a rapid succession of modes of living—the core of us still hangs on, after all, to repeating the ooze-thing, then the fish, then the lizard, then the first furred mammal, every time we're born. We may tinker with lasers or avant-garde political movements—and still be confused that our children aren't tinkering with extensions of the exact same lasers and avant-garde political movements. This may be as good a way as any of explaining my parents' reaction, early on, to rock-and-roll: they were so *sure* it would be *bad* for me. In the late 1940's they walked their neighborhood safely, any time of night. Now Jerry the neighbor's boy walked the dog, just half-a-block down the alley before it was dark out, and returned on his belly with stab-wounds screaming mutely from his back. This has no place in the world they were born to. Although neither does the medical technology that will keep him alive.

*

And: those who came before—how close could Columbus have felt? There are coins and plaques with Hebrew writing that date to the Roman period, unearthed in Tennessee, and we don't know *what* they mean—some plucky, luckless Jewish colony facing raccoon and cougar in the land that would later be Dan'l Boone's? We do know, even if tantalizingly little, of Henry Cabot, and of the early energetic Viking visits—a smithy we've found, with several pounds of slag and

95

pieces of bog-iron, date to the year 1000 and may well be remains of Leif Eirik-son's Vinland settlement. Surely the Norse reached Greenland. From there, the American mainland was striking distance. Landing, connoitering, fingering his missive from the regents of Spain to the Khan of the Indies, freely heaping strings of bells and glass beads into the arms of the natives, what would he have known of those who came before? What do we ever know? In the earliest photos my father is there with his polished-car-grille-smile and his arm around some woman not my mother, although she wears the waist-pinched shoulder-padded dresses of the early 40's my mother also wears in her photos with other men, with "boyfriends" she'd say, and it's all un-thinkable really, all the foldlines on the brains behind those hamming sepia faces might as well be Martian canals. Columbus is trading a bar-ber's scissors for another rumor of gold. Yes, but what's in the ground has far more possibility than gold: a Viking funerary axehead, chips of ruddy ceramic body-parts from what we now call "pre-Columbian" art, the slow descending snow of human and animal bone-chips down to the planet of lava inside this planet, mammal-bone and lizard- and fish- and the petrified slimes of the ooze-thing. Planting his flags in the soil, what could he be like more than a conscious thought, a new and promising surface flurry, above deep-buried Jungian archetypes?

*

"This is no individual acquisition of a seventeen-year-old girl..." Jung is speaking of the symbols in a patient's dream "...it is a collective inheritance, inherited along with the structure of the psyche and therefore to be found at all times and among all peoples." How much of this it's fair for me to constantly place as a shadow under Columbus's feet, I'm not sure. I do know Jung goes on to claim this patient's dream allusions "represent an important part of the Yin idea in Chinese philosophy." This was the new world *he* opened up to Europe—Chinese spiritual life. Tao, he says, is "meaning," or "pur-pose," but also "nothing... Nothing because it does not appear in the world of the senses, but is its organizer." He quotes this wisdom: "If you have insight, you use your inner eye, your inner ear, to pierce to the heart of things, and have no need of intellectual knowledge." (Shen Chou is stirring now—it's nearly night and he feels he's coming alive.) The *I Ching* is a placing of worldly routine "against a cosmic background—the interplay of Yin and Yang." When he shows us that diagrammatic circle, its interlocking paisleys, one white and one black, it's a map of the Earth. And is as accurate as many 15th-century maps of the Earth, or moreso. On top, it's day; a man is taking calculations, trying to go someplace. And on the other side of the world it's night now fully. Shen Chou is at work, on a poem. It's saying he knows he doesn't need to go anywhere; anywhere comes to him.

*

He looks with satisfaction at the scroll he's completed, *The Night Vigil*. The man in it, on the mat-sized meditation table, is so composed! That is, he's made of a few clean, compact strokes, and is weightless, but carries what he needs to—as if he were a cotyledon. And the mountains, and the bamboo, all about. And above it all, where sky blends miscibly into text, Shen Chou's inscription is a stately flock of birds or a kind of lavish weather the heavens let fall in an orderly pour. It's night for Shen Chou as it is for the smaller Shen Chou in his painting, night and what it means of all that opens in the night. And although—it's true—this is the Ming Dynasty and around Shen Chou is a complex mesh of history, political intrigue, technological innovation, fashionability, ritual, scandal, merchantry and military prowess... it's night, prohibitively dark, I can't describe even a single blue-glaze leaf on the Hung-chih style porcelain set on a tax collector's shelf. It's dark. There's nothing. The nothing of Tao. Shen Chou opens, and feels another is present—*his* other, his balance-half. Somewhere on the line of the Earth where Yin meets Yang and they travel along a common border, it's twilight. That is, twin-light. He wishes his own twin well. He writes his line,

I wish to respond with my flute music to the singing
of a distant stream.

*

Jerry, for instance. The neighbor's boy. (It could have been my father who still walks the poodle each night down that same damn alley.) We visit him in his hospital bed, his face is gray. He's 16 and his face is gray. And between him and my father I see another shape take place, a thing named Could-Have-Been-But-Wasn't, and it makes them the halves of a single being, twins of a sort we all are, makes them Others of each other. My father is thinking at least a little of this, and his own face takes on a grayness. Or Hieronymus Müntzer. News travelled slowly. Months passed, and the *Nuremberg Chronicle* published an edition of "the events most worthy of notice from the beginning of the world," but failed to mention Columbus. Unknowingly, Müntzer, a Nuremberg astronomer, wrote a letter in 1493 to King João of Portugal, urging him to seek a sea-route west to the

97

Indies, and giving viable details. Who knows what candescent land-scapes Müntzer nourished inside himself, or what the pitch of his disappointment? The books don't say. But a shape takes place between Columbus and this comic figure, a shadow leaps, a shared conceptual nerve is twanged by happenstance, we're always halves of something larger than any one life—a radio tests its emergency signal and that night, for the first time maybe in many nights, a man and his wife are trying to make a fleshly wholeness of two emphatic halves, and raise that greater Body by sheer caloric rarefaction to someplace it might be, for a moment, a wholeness of even more than their flesh. And I imagine, up to the decent limits in which we imagine such things, how that night, home from the hospital room, my father almost 70 and my mother close to the same, lay down together in their late-life version of just such half-half coupling. Now when I go for my walk each day at dusk, I know I'm in a band of possibility and linkage between a clearcut noon and midnight—how the planet, and our lives we lead on the planet, are like a rabbi in bed, and a love for both God and the full curves of his wife flow into him equally, and mix, and war, the black hat of his calling and the soft white peek of her breast. Our years are world on world, our afternoons are pat-terns attuned to the pacings of Chinese insomniacs. I know all night, in the dripping ticks of time by which a hospital lives, the donor-blood bottles hang upside down. And somewhere else it's bright day; in the caves there, vampire bats by the hundreds of thousands do, and are filled with, the same.

5.

He had brought back ten Indians. The ceremony that interested him most was the baptism, at which the King and Queen graciously consented to act as their godparents. ("Don Juan" remained attached to the royal household and died within two years.) While these baptisms expressed the good intentions of the Sovereigns and, to some extent, of Columbus, it is notorious that the entire Taino race was exterminated within half a century. It may be said, however, that the Tainos had their revenge on Europeans through the present that they innocently brought to Spain in their bloodstream, the spirillum of syphilis.

—arranged from Connell and Morison

A whiff of wet dog
　　　　　dismays the whole of my senses
now—it is only the wolfhound, lolloping in
with his new canary-feathered collar come draggled
from the rain—and it is natural response
to quick a puff of jasmin'ed sniffing-silk
at my nostrils, against the offending odor
of mulchy hound
　　　　　—I used to
run all night on the beach with The People
driving pig and rat and the lizard of my land!
On the ship, when the one called Amadeo had
The Worm, and in its secret travel
up his body showed one night as a white eye
staring out of a black sore, who tell me
who knew to slowly suck it slowly
slowly and so it did not snap, until the entire
handspan of it was out, and I did make a great show
of the chewing and the swallowing. Well
now I sit here with veal
　　　　　on silver plate,
and do not bite twice in a row but Benito attends
to the grease on my chin with a cloth. How very
rapidly we lose ourselves! In order to become
ourselves. Two years ago I last bedonned my body
in feathers and fishbone, when El Admirale paraded us
to his purpose, past the assembled clergy and foppery
of all of Spain—and this with a parrot chained
shitting on each of my shoulders. Now Benito, who helps
in the writing of this (*with many a rare suggestion* —B.)
helps fasten, amid a dozen loving touches, my ruff

from Flanders, and it rests like a risen cream
atop my ivory-with-amber-frippery velvet suit,
with the purple silk stockings and jade-green cavaliers cape.
The ladies, when I raise my gold capped walking cane
as if a spear, and make to impale some blood-encrusted
griffin of their even bloodier fancies,
                                        swoon
or titter in a manner most enchanting, and some
have asked a demonstration of this and other
of what they name my Savage Endowments,
in their chambers, and while the women of The People
have the pinkness of raw meat
I long for miserably, the women here will open with the slow
soft pink of a flower over a season, and this
is also sweet for dandling and etc. Though
who of those composed exquisites will comfort some brown curiosity
in open, day to day? And so I live in this
appendage splendor, here in the apartments
of the dwarves, court witches, jesters and seers,
where my darling angel-faced hip-high shy Benito
is as kind as any wife (*and as beautiful! —B*) and
is available despite his jealous ways, yes
yes Benito and do not cross this out from the record, yes
jealous, and gentle, and with his many, moody,
ministering gifts. El Admirale
                          did not bless this
simple union with Benito, as was my request, and I am hurt,
and yet it was he who made these wonders
mine and so by a next step made these, my
new needs, to match the wonders; and at
my baptism who was radiant with joy for me
to shame the very flambeaux? and so I imagine
a blessing escapes him, like a breath in sleep, perhaps
exactly in his breath while sleeping, and this is truly
of him, if not with his knowing. How I hate
that man!
               and love him—Benito: please—and thinking
of the glory and horror, equal, of my fettered introduction
to these dazzlements, I weep
which as a man of The People I never did, and so it may be that
this half-blinding trickle is the first return of the waters
of my baptism, as the Father said

100

would happen to my enrichment. So: I am brought here
on water, and born here in water, and fear by how
the rain is in my bones tonight I will say farewell of
the same. That such a chill
                              should follow such a flush
of heat! that I encouraged in a waiting-maid of more
than scant allure, and promptly matched. And so my lesson
at the harp was overlong, and led to other strings
they tie beneath the skirts here, wrapping everything, and there
my fingers played the finer tune. But soon
a howling led me out of doors; our sport
was mainly over, and that high commotion coming
from the dark yard seemed a call to me, or something I
once thought was me; it was
                              the wolfhound,
puzzling at a great cage on the far side of the pond, in
which a wolf was brought for some gay entertainment and
paced, lank, leering. We three
only. And I know by how the dog gave out
its howl, and then some whimper, and then a lick at the bars
more tender than not, and then a phlegmy growl, the while
the wolf kept wild silence, how
                              the dog was torn
between its oldest hatred of this skulker,
pack-runner, thiever-on-the-fringes; and
its recognizing brotherhood even older, in a black seed
deep in a backmost doggish sac, that had not
blossomed in the tended soil of men but shivered
as with black petals tensing inside, at every whipcrack
motion of the wolf. I shivered as well. It was the rain,
I think. Each drop seemed whetstone-honed. I cried the dog
away but lingered in the unremitting pour, and
knew no large surprise that lightning of a sudden
brightened everything
                              to show a fourth
had been there, someone standing at the wolf cage in the
shape of a man; and it seemed in my shaking this
naked fellow—for that he was, yes and crazily unkempt—
stared down my eyes, as if perhaps to him they were no
more than corridors, and there espied some buried
seed of my own. And then the light was gone
so he was gone, and I understood how search would come
on nothing. In the pond

                    new water beat with awful fury
for admission to the old; though it was only water,
all of it sufficient and alike, to brooding
goldcarp at the bottom. They say
                                    El Admirale
has made the world two worlds. Oh yes; and he has made me
two-me, and I walked the rain in fuddlement,
how-many-me may populate the dark and step out
fleshed and ready whenever their sign
of arrival is raised in the light.
                                    Of these
and dozenscore conundrums more, I desire
to question the Father when he visits
our gold-and-mother-of-pearl apartments, on some
future day; if only this invasion of the chill
allows me future days. If not, I believe
I will not lack merry company; the fever
of The People has made walking canes
of all my bones, and so has come
to visit here, through me, and is made angry
at the way-stops of our journey, in such degree I see
my gallants and their ladies will be soon enough
in everlasting finery beside me, in whatever
                                            world
we each think flows from this. And I will wait
El Admirale there, when he returns
his last return from sailing, we will both be
in the element of elements, aswim in Time
together, and in Time aswim
(*he raves. It is upon him now, my large, my lovely* —B.)

6.

A Columbian Sonnet

By the spring, Columbus felt well enough to travel, provided he could ride a mule; a horse's gait was too rough for him. On May 19, 1506, he ratified his final will. Columbus had the ill fortune to die at the moment when his discoveries were little valued, and his personal fortunes and expectations were at their lowest ebb. He had written: "The world has ever treated men ill. Today it casts me down most cruelly; but the hope in Him who created all things sustains me, for His help has ever been at hand. Once before I was downcast and He said unto me: 'Man of little faith, fear not, be comforted. I am with thee.'" The official court chronicle mentioned neither death nor funeral.
                    —arranged from Connell and Morison

1) An hour behind the serial gifts of his mule, with their toolshed

4) jaws, the beetles had emptied the road of its droppings.
   Even a mule's pace enflamed his buttocks. It was *this*
   world's transport, always, that beset him: severed
   mainmasts, hellish military hikes. But as for transport

9) to the next, he had no doubt. If some said beetle,
   worm and maggot were the vehicles
   by which we cross the threshold
   —and he'd seen these at their skills—to him, the final
   voyage of all was incorporeal. He wrote: "God the Lord is
   present, and will take account of my services."
   And the poet Todros Ben Judah Abulafia (1247–1298)
   wrote: "Look, how the vultures of Fortune prey
   On me, and devour my flesh all day.

2) (And if they afflict me on this Earth...so?
   My soul will rejoice in the world to come.)"

7.

Mandeville: 1356. The Orlando series: 1483–1532.
And: "there may very likely exist
human beings like ourselves,
probably with strange costumes and
still stranger manners"

*

—Robert Goddard, on possible extraterrestrial life:

*

1902. Who climbed the ledge
to the cherry tree. This was with his body, in 1899. And then
who kept on going, into the sky, and this was with
whatever neuron-crackling travels from the body in that moment
of formative understanding we might call "inspiration."
Who was 17 on the smooth-skinned chocolate limb of a cherry,
in burnt-orange (it was October), in New England,
with his mother wheezing t.b. and his own breath maybe just
this hazy side of being gray in the cooling afternoon air,
who sees, who out of nowhere and being nobody, sees
in the last official days of the 19th century, that
travel to Mars is possible. October 19. Travel to Mars

*

is possible. The planet hangs in his eye more red,
more real, than any cherry that tree will ever bloom.
Who every year for his life will stop
to celebrate that day, that "Anniversary Day." Who
leads his life: solid- and liquid-fueled rocket flight,
trajectory, apogee, ultraviolet observation of stars,
magnesium signals, solar-powered rocket engines.
To get to Mars. Who was the first. Who saw it, huge in possibility.
Who led his life. To get to Mars. Who said "God
pity a one-dream man." Who fantasized a means
of sending human genetic material
into space, and there at some distant time

recombining, producing a generation of people
whose breaths beneath a sky of 2 or 17 or no moons,
would be ultimate flags with which to substantiate
claim over ultimate soil.

*

I still have Columbus: emerald-green
construction paper. He's holding that solid, emerald-green
generic flag in an attitude so
proprietary, showfull and triumphant, it incorporates,
already, Iwo Jima and the moon. Then I'd go
on to be me, in the stepping-out-of and -into that's like the
wave of walking Muybridge captured
photographing steps of human movement, only
over years. Through all of this

*

it passes down. Through years of nights on the gravel roof
with Duke the Dumb Dog running perfect Copernican
circles around me and then it was bedtime. Ronnie
Schaeffer stole my glasses—he belonged to a gang
called the River Rats; with knives. Through my bar mitzvah.
Through the first death (Grandma Nettie, who was always a shadow
on Daddy's skin and when she rose to Heaven I could see
that shadow go correspondingly smaller until at the Gate it
wholly vanished). It passes down, it expands or diminishes or
it changes kind, but always it passes down. Through the first
intense embarrassment, through the first ungainly fuck
and through the last. On a poem. With a drink.
In a '59 Chevy (the exhaust was 3 rigged Coke cans).
Out of Utah, where the loneliness completed its terrible orbit
of my body every 24 hours—I could feel it, punching time
in the switchback tracks of the wrists. To New York.
With Elaine in those soul-crazy days in Vermont when
even the nights seemed so bright, every scrap of shadow disappeared
like a roach under something. But those sorts of days
never last. From each revision,
wadded like cubism balls in the trash. On a high.
By the classics. Plugged in. Played out. With every
stacked amino acid making sub-shape out of shapelessness, it

105

passes down, that internalized paper Columbus saying
Go now with its indicating green hand,
though it's frayed, though it's partially discolored: *Go,
and do your own small version of what I
did first, and forever, to scale.*

It passes down. On his return, Columbus passed through
the village Trujillo, where
"an illiterate young swineherd, Francis Pizarro" most
likely gawked at him, and then
through Medellín, "where Cortés, at that time eight years old,
undoubtedly saw him." He said Mars to them,
though not in any known language. He became a sign,
a pointing. I was reading science-fiction
on the gravel roof in 1961, and pioneers
were brave in bubble-domes below the twin Mars moons,
and when they died they'd be the elements
the future inhaled, though *they* breathed only
a virginal, canistered air that I saw as a matrix,
and wanted to climb toward. It became
language, not planets. But both are worlds,
with atmospheres, with gravities. We

reach that ledge, that stony ledge. We leap from that gaunt, fall cherry.
With each complete inch of interlocked Muybridge-step it
passes down, and what *are* we, if not brief,
personal versions of Goddard's process:
genetic material,
carried, each day of us, farther.
Go, and do.

- -

When a waterspout "the width of a cask" approached his already near-decimated caravels, Columbus grabbed his sword and with it traced a massive cross upon the sky. Evidently it worked. Invisible angels (of protection, in this case) must have thronged the air back then, and entered through that aerial with amazingly clear reception.

Today, Columbus's house in Valladolid is a small, poorly tended museum: Casa de Colón. There are few visitors. Most of its lights remain off. And raised from the roof is a TV antenna, the elderly caretaker catching whatever high-hemmed secular angels fire derringers or jiggle-dance in latex between his taciturn tours. It's interesting to think Neil Armstrong's first step onto the moon might have, like a flash of attracted St. Elmo's fire, played around this antenna—this mast of what's left—and so entered the dark of the place in a benedictory spirit. At least it's possible. I hope it occurred.

And it's interesting to think of Robert Goddard being in Worcester, Massachusetts (as he was—it was his hometown, and he became a professor of physics at Clark University there) when Freud and Jung passed through in 1909, and gave their first detailed discussion in English of psychoanalysis. Goddard would have been a young physics graduate student then. Would he have attended? At least it's possible.

He might have been there in the audience, that man of nozzles, calipers, sidereal calculations, tables of phases down to the thousandths-place, vector formulae, fuel tanks. He might have faced Jung. And the talk went like this: "Yin... the stars... the other... Yang... the self... the dream... the world-dream."

*

And Shen Chou wrote:
Off a stony ledge, a path narrow and long soars into the void.

ABOUT THE AUTHOR

ALBERT GOLDBARTH is the author of numerous collections, of which *Jan. 31* (1974) was nominated for the National Book Award and *Original Light* (1983) was the recipient of the Texas Institute of Letters Prize. His poems have appeared in most major journals and many anthologies (most recently, *The Harvard Book of Contemporary Poetry*, edited by Helen Vendler), and have over the years found support in grants from the National Endowment for the Arts and a Guggenheim Fellowship. Born in Chicago in 1948, Mr. Goldbarth now lives in Austin, Texas and teaches at the University of Texas.

ONTARIO REVIEW PRESS POETRY SERIES